# SHILLAY AND THE SEALS

*by the same author*

ISLAND GOING
QUEST FOR THE GRIFFON
GROWING APPLES

# SHILLAY
# AND THE SEALS

Robert Atkinson

COLLINS and HARVILL PRESS
London, 1980

Map of the Sound of Harris
based upon the Ordnance Survey map
with the permission of
the Controller of Her Majesty's Stationery Office
Crown Copyright Reserved

© 1980 Robert Atkinson
ISBN 0 00 262763 9

Photoset in English Times by
T. J. Press (Padstow) Ltd,
Made and printed in Great Britain by
William Collins Sons & Co Ltd, Glasgow
for Collins, St James's Place and
Harvill Press, 30A Pavilion Road, London SW1

*For Sally*

# CONTENTS

Sections of photographs between pages 40 and 41, 88 and 89, 120 and 121, 136 and 137.

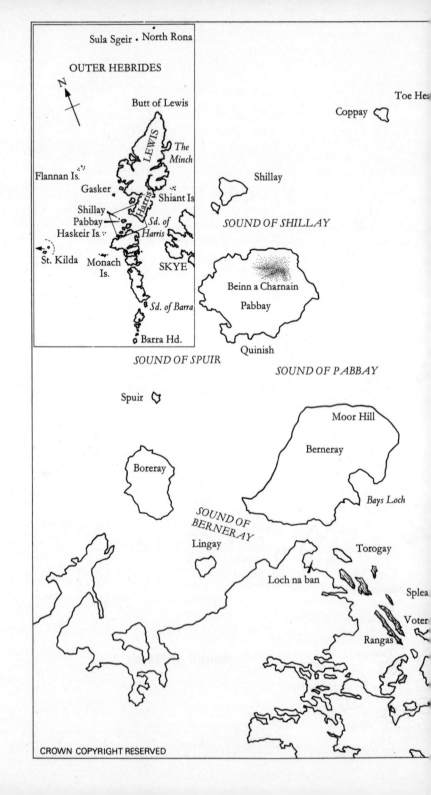

SOUND OF SHILLAY

Shillay

Coppay

Toe Hea

SOUND OF PABBAY

Beinn a Charnain

Pabbay

Quinish

SOUND OF SPUIR

Spuir

Moor Hill

Berneray

Bays Loch

Boreray

SOUND OF BERNERAY

Lingay

Torogay

Loch na ban

Splea

Voter

Rangas

**OUTER HEBRIDES**

Sula Sgeir • North Rona

N

Butt of Lewis

LEWIS

The Minch

Flannan Is.

Gasker

Harris

Shiant Is

Shillay
Pabbay
Haskeir Is.

Sd. of Harris

St. Kilda

Monach Is.

SKYE

Sd. of Barra

Barra Hd.

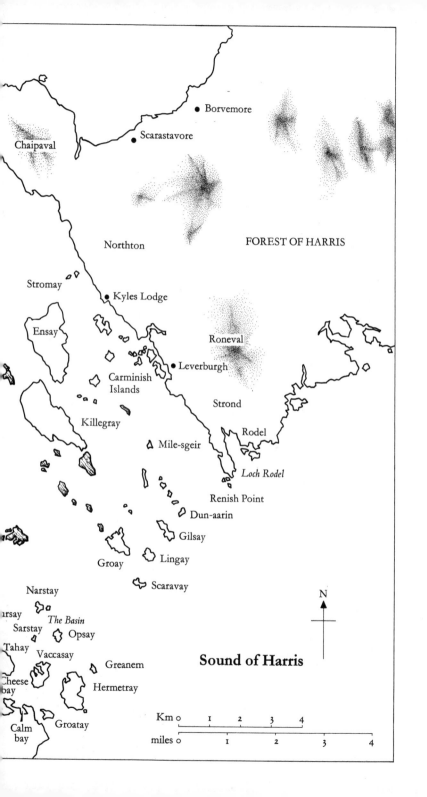

Borvemore

Scarastavore

Chaipaval

FOREST OF HARRIS

Northton

Stromay

Kyles Lodge

Ensay

Roneval

Carminish
Islands

Leverburgh

Killegray

Strond

Rodel

Mile-sgeir

*Loch Rodel*

Renish Point

Dun-aarin

Gilsay

Groay

Lingay

Scaravay

Narstay

N

rsay

*The Basin*

Sarstay

Opsay

Tahay

Vaccasay

Greanem

Cheese
bay

Hermetray

Calm
bay

Groatay

**Sound of Harris**

Km

1      2      3      4

miles

1           2           3           4

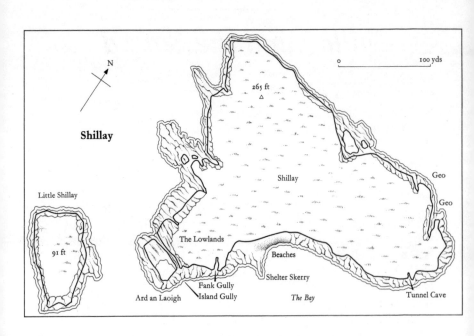

N

100 yds

265 ft

Shillay

Shillay

Little Shillay

91 ft

Geo

Geo

The Lowlands

Beaches

Shelter Skerry

Fank Gully

Ard an Laoigh   Island Gully

The Bay

Tunnel Cave

# ONE

---◆---

# *Shillay and the Sound*

Shillay, one small island of the innumerable Hebrides, stands out a little from the long line of the Outer Isles. It lies at the Atlantic end of the Sound of Harris, where the Sound widens and loses itself into the ocean. The water deepens and changes from pellucid green to deep Atlantic slate. Shillay is the last of the land.

The small lonely island with its rounded hill shares the worlds of ocean and of shallow sound. Its northern and western face is cliff-bound and gives to the ocean; the full Atlantic swell ends its run at Shillay's cliff-foot. But hill and cliff-crest fall the other way to a landward shore that belongs to the Sound. The rocks and shingle are round the corner from the Atlantic and seaweed swirls comfortably. There is even a little strip of white shell sand, backed by a miniature, marram-fringed cliff of trickling sand, a last outlier from the white seaside acres of Berneray and Ensay and Killegray in the body of the Sound. Their dunes and machair roll a mile at a time; Shillay has a token pocket handkerchief.

The island is near enough a triangle in shape, with its hill summit rising to 265 feet at the north-west point; its longest measurement is just half a mile, across the base facing the Sound, and the area is a little over one hundred acres. It has never been inhabited but sheep are pastured there. Little Shillay, or Shillay Beg, lies alongside, separated by a narrow boiling channel; it is a precipitous black rock but covered with flowers in summertime. Grey seals resort to Shillay every autumn and haul ashore to breed. Their immemorial coming holds Shillay to the ocean, and the lack of any trace of human habitation plainly shows that the island has never been tamed towards the Sound.

For a ship coming in from the Atlantic, Shillay and the bare battleship rock of Coppay, further over towards Harris, mark the opening to the Sound and to the tortuous channel leading through to the Minch. The Sound of Harris is the only way through the long barrier of the Outer Isles, until the Sound of Barra opens another gap, but too near the southern end to be useful for navigation. Lewis and Harris lie solid for sixty miles to north and east, the Uists and Benbecula straggle forty miles to south and west, the sandy fords amongst them as impassable as dry land. Big ships go round the Butt of Lewis or Barra Head, as ever; the Sound has never been open to more than small vessels. A rusty old Aberdeen trawler might steam through to fish westwards, leaving a shimmer of heat behind her blackened funnel, or a rare summertime yacht bound for St Kilda. The *Northern Lights* relief ship was a regular visitor for many years, on her way to serve the Flannan Isles, or coming in once a year to paint the iron beacons and the solitary buoy. Usually there is only some loggish small boat out from Berneray or Harris, slowly moving in and out of sight among the rocks.

There have been busier times. The tall mid-Victorian beacons were built to answer a need, and for the half-century that the old steamships *Dunara Castle* and *Hebrides* worked the St Kilda run they regularly navigated the Sound. It was from the deck of the *Hebrides*, coming back from St Kilda in August 1938, that I first saw Shillay. It was the first island the ship came to as she closed the land, then only a name from the map and soon left astern. Six miles further on the ship passed the gaunt beacons of Red Rock and Sgeir Volinish, then held close along the Harris shore, then turned hard over, first one way and then the other, following the dog-leg channel off Leverburgh, and then on clear to Rodel. She stopped for me off Rodel Loch while I and my belongings piled into the waiting motor boat. She steamed on into the Minch, as calm as a millpond on that warm August evening, and I went ashore to Rodel with my head full of islands and birds.

She and her sister ship had one more season in the islands; so did I and in the process I bought for a song a twenty year old, 8-ton, near derelict fishing boat named *Heather*. Then the war came. The old ships never went back to St Kilda and within a few years first one and then the other had made their last voyages to the breaker's yard.

I was back again at Rodel nine years later. The war was over, the *Heather* was refurbished out of all recognition, re-engined and spruce in fresh paint, and on her way on an expedition to St Kilda. We should see how the deserted island had fared during the war years and we hoped to carry out a census of the immemorial inhabitants, the birds. The year before we had had the boat out for a preliminary fortnight and had been to North Rona; this time we had the month of June and all the west coast before us.

John Naish – old school friend and travelling companion in many enterprises – and I sailed from Stornoway to collect the rest of the party: first across the Minch to Wester Ross, to pick up James Fisher, ornithologist, from Achiltibuie Pier, then down to Skye to find Frank Fraser Darling, ecologist, waiting on the beach of Kilmaluag Bay. But the engine was playing up – I was still a beginner with it – and we were stumbling along on three cylinders with a filthy exhaust. We crossed the Minch again and dropped the naturalists with food and a tent on the Shiant Isles, and went back to Stornoway in a calm night. We returned next evening, having consulted Bob Scott, the marine engineer, but the breeze had freshened from the wrong quarter and a northerly swell was setting straight on to the steep shingle landing beach. It was no place to be; we anchored and kept the doubtful engine running. John managed to get ashore in the dinghy, and scampered away barefoot in the wind and rain, to see how the others were getting on. No tent! – they had found the empty cottage unlocked and were sitting in front of a roaring driftwood fire, correcting proofs; they looked up rather crossly through their specs. We left them and got across to Loch

Brollum in Lewis for the rest of the night. Next day we tried again but it was no better, and the engine remained a nagging worry. We lay overnight in East Loch Tarbert, Harris. By next morning the wind was south-westerly and freshening but in the best quarter for the Shiants beach; and this time we managed to get the naturalists off the island.

We set off down the coast of Harris on 8 June 1947, and slowly and miserably punched southwards all the afternoon into a drenching head sea. Fortunately the engine was manful at last, a steady racket down below for hour after hour. An occasional storm petrel followed the wake but finding only a whiff of paraffin smoke each sheered off in turn. Eventually we got to Rodel, and, determined to find the ultimate sheltered corner, went far into the weedy and sandy recesses of Rodel Loch, where the chart no longer gave soundings, and not unexpectedly took the ground. A man rowed out from a croft on the shore and asked if we had mistaken the way through the Sound. It was not as bad as that and indeed at this stranger's stage we were treating the Admiralty's *West Coast of Scotland Pilot* with all the deference due to its measured and biblical style. In an hour or two the tide began to make, the laminaria streamed the other way and the oil film pumped from the bilges spread back round the boat. At half-tide we removed to Rodel Basin and anchored in a more seamanlike manner. By now the *Heather* had shown Frank Darling the limits of his seafaring endurance and he sensibly withdrew to the hotel and retired from the voyage. We lay in the windy, unsummerly weather and got the cabin dried out.

The Sound of Harris is ten miles through from Minch to Western Ocean, from Renish Point to Toe Head along the bold Harris shore, and seven or eight miles wide from Harris to the indeterminate bogs and lochs of North Uist on the other side. In variety of land and water these contrasting shores enclose an area not to be matched anywhere else in the British Isles. The biggest island is Berneray, three and a half miles long, the smallest a boulder above high water. Nearly all the detail of Hebridean country is gathered within the for-tuitous maze of islands and islets and reefs and rocks. The deep fiord-like sea lochs of eastern Lewis are missing and so are the ferny freshwater lochs of the Uists, but all the rest is there, and changing from island to island. The sweet-smelling open space of flowery machair and shell sand is contrasted again and again with the sour black roll of peat. The drab acres called 'rough grazing' that blanket so much of Scotland, crown some of the islands. There are islets deep in woody heather never burnt and close cropped slopes of crowberry where the barnacle geese graze in wintertime. Even rare trees, rowan and aspen, perch in short landward cliffs, and there are steep sea-walls with ledges whitened by seabirds. Buzzards and terns, gulls and mergansers all find their place to live and to nest. There are otters' holts in the peat and boulder shores infested with rats.

For the seals the Sound is as much a way through the barrier line of the Outer Isles as it is for ships; the seals keep over to the Uist side away from habitation and drift down their known submarine galleries among the weed.

The Sound has a Gunwale Channel and a Calm Bay, a Grey Horse and a Cabbage Group. The Norse names of the islands run in a string, not only the main lands of Berneray, Pabbay, Ensay, Killegray but also Torogay and Tahay, Vaccasay and Sursay, Sarstay and Opsay; and even Narstay. In one place the ebb tide creates from a sheet of open water a straight narrow canal a mile long, a cutting in the rock with steep walls of wet seaweed rising close on either side.

Like the waters of the Sound, the islands have known busier days. The village of Berneray is still populous but a couple of cattlemen on Killegray and the lonely shepherd of Pabbay are all the rest of the inhabitants. The deep pastures of Ensay and Killegray and Pabbay are still fully stocked, and sheep are still boated to and from the unlikeliest islets. Fisheries and their shore stations have come and gone. The island peat banks have been worked and abandoned, the drystone bothies are fallen into casual heaps, the herring bone patterns of lazybeds have long been smoothed with turf. Once the larger islands on the Uist side were all 'inhabit and manurit' and the string of islets along the Harris shore were cultivated wherever a pocket of soil rested among the rocks: boats of long ago moving crabwise across the tide, serving the tilled patches of oats and barley and potatoes. Here is the white empty beach of Ensay where Martin Martin set out on his famous voyage to St Kilda: 'we embark'd at the Isle *Esay* in *Harries* the 29th of *May*, at Six in the afternoon, 1697, the Wind at S.E. . . .' Martin Martin was a native of Skye and an intrepid traveller in the Western Isles. His two books *A Late Voyage to St Kilda* . . . (1698) and *A Description of the Western Isles of Scotland* (1703), remain the only, and highly entertaining, works on the subject at this time. It was his *Description* that inspired Johnson and Boswell's tour of the Hebrides.

At the back of the beach stands Ensay mansion house, dank and deserted, and upstairs remains a great four-poster bed hung with mouldering velvet, silent within the stone walls. Along the beach any little scratching at the face of the dunes soon uncovers blackened sand, burnt shells and bones and shards of grey pottery, the meals of two thousand years ago. A standing stone rubbed by cattle marks the summit of a mound, a chapel stands locked and empty, the ancient burial ground is a row of flagstones sticking out of the cropped turf.

Twice a day the Atlantic tide pulses through to the Minch, running like a river through the narrow channels, seeping and brimming to the last recess, then turning back and falling to leave basins and lagoons running with waterfalls. There can have been hardly any change since the last ice sheet withdrew; a slow building of peat, some smoothing of rock and shifting of sand by wind and weather, but no more. Human activities have rearranged some stones but the surface scratches are hardly more than sheep tracks. The Sound keeps its personality as the skies and colours change, and the water brims or falls.

The local men's knowledge of the channels and rocks passes from generation to generation; anyone who does possess the Admiralty chart of the Sound keeps it put away in a drawer. I spent ten years exploring and learning the Sound; it became my chosen place in all the Hebrides. Year after year the old *Heather* was to plug down from Stornoway to turn on Renish Point and open the fairway. I anticipated none of this as we lay for the first time in Rodel Basin; an arrival that turned out to be a threshold for both boat and crew.

We lay the night at Rodel and next day moved up the fairway towards Leverburgh in a sunny breeze. Ten miles ahead, at the Atlantic end of the Sound, the swell showed breaking white on the battleship prow of Coppay. The water was blue and green, there was a gleam of white beaches among the littered islets and rocks with their grassy tops and seaweed fringes. The east end of Coppay lay correctly in line with Suem, Cook Rock buoy was coming up to port, all was in order for a clear run up to Jane Tower on the starboard bow.

'A vessel might, in case of necessity, proceed through the Sound, or to a safe anchorage in it, but it is not advisable to attempt this without local knowledge, on account of the strong tidal streams and numerous shoals.' The *Heather* was an eight-ton Fyfie, thirty-six feet by twelve, and drew four feet aft – sometimes a vessel and sometimes a boat. Study of the *Pilot* soon led to impatience; it allowed almost no inshore navigation 'except', in its own refrain, 'by boats with local knowledge'. This status we set out to acquire as soon as possible; we passed Cook Rock, we rounded Jane Tower with the shore beacons in line ahead, and turned in to tie up to the surviving half of Leverburgh pier.

In the village we took Simon Mackenzie the merchant's last drum of paraffin and fuelled to capacity. The weather forecast was good and in the evening we sailed for St Kilda, being the first boat to go out since the war. A crowd of men and children watched us away.

The rest of the channel turned out to be a pleasant exercise in pilotage, between the Harris shore on one hand and the Saghay group of islands on the other. First along the shore comes the bottom-up wreck of an Admiralty trawler which failed to turn in time, then Ru Smearinish, 'moderately bold', then Kyles Lodge, a white house alone on the shore, a seamark, but to become nearly as familiar as my own home.

17

Next come the two beacons, Volinish, red, to be left to port, and Red Rock, black, to starboard; once past and they are put in line astern. This bearing clears Colla Sgeir to port, Girls Rock, the Irishman and Temple rocks to starboard. The promontory now in sight on the Harris shore is Bretasker or Cape Difficulty, though why so named I never discovered. Once Toe Head is open all the dangers are past, 'vessels can steer out to sea', and only Shillay and Coppay remain to break the western horizon.

We passed between the two, at eleven in the evening, overcast, and entered into the grey hills of the Atlantic.

We left the Outer Isles grey and cloud capped. Coppay lay low and black under the twin hills of Toe Head; Little Shillay opened southwards of Shillay and they stood apart; Pabbay, the next island inwards, preserved its outline of a classical flattened pyramid as the bearing slowly changed. The islands dwindled in steady rain; we watched them to the last to learn how the landmarks would look when we should raise them coming back again from seaward. At last smudgy sketch showed them strung out in line.

In fact we were back again four days later, driven out of Village Bay, St Kilda, by a south-easterly blow; we came all the way back to Harris rather than dodge indefinitely under the lee of the St Kilda cliffs. This was a beastly passage in a steep breaking swell and bleak as winter. We got too far to the north until Pabbay's pyramid and then the Shillays showed the way in.

Next time was better; we went out by the Sound of Pabbay, between Shillay and Pabbay, and left astern blue hills and rosy piled cumulus. St Kilda was in sight even from Shillay and the swell was down. But it was another night passage with an uncertain engine and elderly gear and then continuous anchor watch to be kept at St Kilda. We had a nasty time in a gale there and 'too much dry mouth on this trip' I noted, when finally we got back and the *Heather* was once again rubbing gently against Leverburgh pier. Next morning the Sound lay glassy under a pale sky and terns from the near islets loitered overhead. James Fisher hurried off to some distant conference; John Naish and I were left uncommitted, with a few more days to spare.

We did not go to Shillay, there would be no seals there in the summertime, but I did learn that the tenant was Simon Mackenzie himself, the merchant. He had the island from the Board of Agriculture and although as a grazier his serious preoccupation was with Ensay, he did put a few sheep on Shillay. They put them on in the autumn to overwinter and it was then that they would see the seal pups on the shore. That was when I wanted to go, was half planning to go, but nothing was fixed. We came to know Murdo Macdonald, lobsterman, of the *Bluebell*, who had already let us have another drum of paraffin; he agreed to do the ferrying to Shillay, if weather permitted. It was not his ground and he had never been there. If anyone fished lobsters around Shillay, it would be boats from Berneray.

We entertained and were entertained by Leslie and Margaret Lomas of Kyles Lodge, the only English residents; they made the splendidly generous suggestion that I should use their house as a base. Rodel had seemed the only possible, yet inconveniently distant place. Shillay was rising fast on my horizon, though when we left the Sound the island was still familiar only as a seamark. But I was already hoping to be able to come north again in the autumn and camp out on Shillay for a week, to see what went on. The number of seals breeding on the island was not known, and I had a brief to take photographs for the New Naturalist series of books.

From Leverburgh pier we boated across the mouth of the Obbe to the uninhabited shore on the other side. Two men were working at a peat bank on a midgy evening, cutting and throwing up the peats to dry; 'there's a lot of work in the peats before you will get them home'. We saw more of the man who called himself piermaster, whose numerous children all issued from one small hut, and who went barefoot and had perfect feet. We saw much of the feet, as the children sat and dangled them over the pier, watching the *Heather* below. (I saw them grow up and take to shoes, and go away to work.) The solitary shepherd of Pabbay was having a spell ashore, after nine months alone on his island. He was pointed out to us as we went to Rodel, lying on the grass at the roadside, the bar having closed, and smiling on those who passed.

We explored and went bird's nesting on all the islets within dinghy range, and surveyed a locally known channel for the *Heather*. The township's stock bull, a magnificent Highlander on loan from the Board of Agriculture, had been put to graze on the islet called Suem an t-Sruith. He offered a variety of craggy silhouettes as we rowed round; next day he was towed back by the horns to the mainland shore.

All the wooden and greater part of Leverburgh pier was steadily being demolished and the timber converted. A temporary sawmill had been set up on the peninsula behind the pier, and the timber was going all over Lewis and Harris. This was the site of the fish factories built by Lord Leverhulme, the last of the great improvers. He held that the seas of the Hebrides were richer by far than the land; his trawlers and drifters would have direct access to the Atlantic fishing grounds; if necessary he would put a light on every rock in the Sound of Harris. He would build a breakwater to shelter the pier and deepen the entrance into the Obbe, to make an inner harbour. The trappings of seaside industry arrived. Two great steel and corrugated-iron buildings arose, a row of houses, lighthouses, a water tower, a light railway, a road, the pier itself; and the old township of Obbe became Leverburgh. When he died in 1925 it all came to an instant end.

Ozymandias! – the colossal wreck still remaining was the gaunt skeleton of one of the great sheds. A couple of newly-weds had built a shack in one corner and pushed a chimney pipe out through the rusty wall. The other shed had already been dismantled and re-erected as a Stornoway garage. Half-built houses remained as on the day Lord Leverhulme died; and still do. The sawmill inside its prison compound of barbed wire and pier piles gave off a delicious smell of pine sawdust. On one side lay the tidal Obbe, brackish at the head and full of old bicycles, its narrow entrance by the pier still only passable to a small boat at high water. All round the ruins grew a profusion of orchids: butterfly, spotted, the various marsh, and all their brilliant hybrids.

We stayed as long as we could and then made the voyage back to Stornoway in one hop; another night passage.

# TWO

## *Island Idyll*

In wind and rain the Sound of Harris loses its singularity and becomes drab rock and grey sea with the rest of the Hebrides.

So it was when I got back again to Leverburgh in the autumn of the same year, 1947. It had been such a brilliant sharp morning when I set out on the long drive north, leaving behind all the colouring leaves and ripening fruit of England; but I arrived to blowing drizzle and a gale warning. Simon Mackenzie next morning thought it was still early for seal pups – it was the 27th of September but in any case the weather was quite unfit for any attempt at Shillay. Murdo Macdonald's house was up a bit from sea level, just high enough to raise the thin white strip of sand on Shillay, nearly ten miles away; through a glass and on a clear day he had been able to make out some black dots against the white – 'I think they might be seals' – but now the Sound was lost in blowing rain and mist. I spent the first of a good many afternoons in an armchair at Kyles Lodge.

For more than a fortnight the rain rained and the gale warnings were monotonously renewed. The sea barely began to die down before it was whipped up again. There was no comfort here, no trees, no shelter, no lane or dell, all lay bare as a board.

The desultory work of the islands went on, I alone was nobbled by the weather. Haymaking and harvest were still unfinished, sad wisps of hay hung along the wire fences and

22

thin sheaves of oats were being carried from minute patches of stubble. Simon Mackenzie was ferrying fat cattle from Ensay to the traditional landing beach at Kyles; the bullocks and 'hyfers' were driven up planks from the well of the big boat, and tipped over the side. They seemed to be a long time under water, then they surfaced and swam ashore, urged on by much Gaelic shouting; they stood dripping as soon as they got a foothold. At Leverburgh pier the old *Challenger*, a converted trawler, still made regular calls. She unloaded wheat straw – baled full length for thatching – and hay and fencing wire and posts, cement, dry provisions, but the only export was empty beer barrels. When she sailed, the sight of the little black steamer threading a way through the rocks, streaming her low trail of smoke to leeward, could have been more than a century old, a print of some early steamboat out from the Clyde.

Leverburgh's milk supply came from Inverness: by rail across Scotland, by mail steamer across the Minch and by sixty mile bus ride from Stornoway. The churns were put down at the roadside below the post office; the customers came with their various vessels and the post mistress delegated one of them to serve out the milk. If there was any left over a visitor could get some. While the bus waited at Leverburgh, it was used as a haircutting saloon.

At Rodel Hotel the staple fare was cold mutton and boiled potatoes, preceded by soup swimming with barley and followed by prunes and custard. In these days of short supply, prunes were a rarity, even Mackenzie's store had none. Round the back of the hotel, outside the bar, bedraggled hens stood on one leg in the lee of stacks of empty beer crates – microcosm of the Hebrides. The next nearest bar was either fifteen miles on by sea to Lochmaddy or twenty-five miles back by road to Tarbert.

I went to Rodel for its telephone: James Fisher had organized an ambitious three day aerial survey of all the known or possible Scottish and Welsh grey seal colonies: within the area of western Harris and Uist the flying boat was due to cover Gasker and Taransay, Shillay, Haskeir, the

Monach Isles, Causamul and Deasker: I was to be given a report on Shillay from the air, if radio contact could be achieved. (There then existed an Advisory Committee on Airborne Research Facilities; not surprisingly the idea of flying naturalists about in service aircraft did not last long but on the marvellous Rockall Flight of the previous summer I had been one of the ever-grateful passengers.)

The Sunderland duly arrived one wet day, flying steadily up the Sound. Leslie Lomas, a keen radio ham, desperately tried to call it and the aircraft was trying to call him, but they failed to hear each other. The flying boat roared low past Kyles Lodge and headed out to sea, for Gasker; later we saw it circling round Shillay in the rain.

This attempt at counting seals from the air turned out to be unreliable but it did reveal an unexpectedly large colony on Gasker with possibly up to a hundred and fifty pups. By contrast the observers counted only six newly born pups on Shillay and three in the middle skerry of Taransay Glorigs. This information came next day by telegram, but, the weather being what it was, remained of academic interest.

When the clouds did part, sunlight flooded the island in an extraordinary white brilliance. Hebridean sunshine is incandescent, because the air is completely clean; it is halfway to moonlight; the nearest that mainland light ever gets to it is April sunshine after rain. Below the dark pall of cloud the ground was alight.

The orchids by the pier were long gone and the near islets lifeless, but in sudden sunshine the bleached sea debris of crabs' legs and shells and driftwood and the heaps of enormous iron bollards awaiting removal, all stood in surrealist clarity. The driftwood scrubbed by wind and rain was white as bone. The seaweed along the shore had a fungoid brilliance of colour and beyond the sea was tumbling blue and white.

In the Forest of South Harris, a tree-less deer forest, the line of telegraph posts marched away to infinity, each pole with a white sunlit line drawn down one side; 'there is not a shrub of Wood to be seen in all the Forrest', said Martin. The stony waste lay in a detail of Pre-Raphaelite sharpness, fit setting for a tethered Scapegoat. It was enough to sit and look.

I went on filling in time: worked on the car; had a nice fire on the beach and boiled out an oily jerrican for fresh water; went lobstering with Angus, the Kyles' factotum, home from the war in his Commando's beret; marched with him for miles over the windblown moors and actually shot a brace of grouse. The juniper bushes growing in drier places there were wholly prostrate, clinging tightly to every contour of ground or rock. Along the shore stray plants of scabious and tormentil and even a few field gentians were still in flower and in boggy places the rain-wetted seed heads of asphodel were bright as orange peel. I climbed Roneval, the highest local hill, and saw St Kilda again. I lay in wait for rabbits on the Saghay islets; I packed and repacked my goods and carefully hoarded stores; and walked interminably. But it is sad to say that in bad weather in the Hebrides there is no pleasure and nothing to see except blowing mist. When tourism began to expand in later years visitors in Stornoway were apt to complain that there was nothing to do except walk round Woolworths. Fishermen are different.

At last, and after nineteen days of waiting, it was my turn. 'Before the weather forecast there is a warning' – not, for a change, of west to south-west gales in sea areas Hebrides etc., etc., but of ground frost overnight; 'wind light variable, fair, visibility good.' I hurried to see Murdo Macdonald and his mate, another Angus. They came round the same afternoon in the *Bluebell*, towing a dinghy; we loaded up and were away at four o'clock.

The *Bluebell* was no ocean greyhound. She was a beamy double-ended open boat of nineteen foot keel, powered with a little Morris paraffin engine; she had been built in Skye and was literally a hundred years old; some of her timbers were still original.

Coming out against the full flood tide and towing a heavy dinghy was a slow business. The sea was quiet but the swell kept on hiding our small island in the distance. When Pabbay was close to port, Coppay away to starboard and Shillay straight ahead, Murdo was in strange water. As a lobsterman from Leverburgh he worked the Harris side of the Sound, out to Coppay, round Toe Head and beyond to Taransay and offlying Taransay Glorigs – a horrible collection of rocks above and below water; 'a bugger of a place', said Murdo.

As we got nearer and lifted the beach we could see it was dotted with dark spots, seals perhaps or lumps of tangle or rocks. There were white dots of sheep above. Nearer still and most of the sheep turned into white coated seal pups – the grass was littered with them. All the low ground westwards from the hill was littered with seals young and old, and where the land began to rise seals had worked the hillside into a black mud slide. The beach itself was thick with big beasts – a herd. Murdo was excited with it all; he stopped well offshore, to put the boat business out of mind for a minute or two – 'I want to have a look at this'. There were big heads bobbing all round the boat now – 'look at that, look at that one'.

The stampede began as we anchored. The seals on the grass began urging themselves downhill towards the shore, it was like a rabbit warren on the move. There seemed to be hundreds. They came with an extraordinary lolloping gait, the front flippers rowing like oars, hind limbs trailing as useless flaps behind. They crossed the beach and the rocks and boulders on either side, plunged and submerged into the safety of the sea. They came bulls and cows together; their coats were dry and showed a variety of colour, blacks and browns, greys and dapples. The beach cleared first, the sand was left marked as if tractors had been playing on it.

The waves sluiced mildly up the beach, there would be no trouble over landing. We piled my stuff into the dinghy, rowed to the windward end of the sand, jumped out and pulled her in. We unloaded in a rush, then pulled the boat up clear. Murdo wasn't going to miss the chance of a look around.

One or two pups on the sand had been born since last high water, the sand was still stained with blood. There were pups at every stage from fat dappled grey barrels, with their baby coats shed round them, to newest born, still wet, umbilical cords hanging fresh, afterbirths nearby; even at that age they were ready to open a toothless pink mouth and try a baby snarl. The air was full of their cries, so searchingly like the cry of a human baby; they lay helpless and abandoned. Nearly all the adults had headed precipitately for the sea as we arrived but a few cows were left, especially in inland peaty pools. The pups by these wallows were dirty and plastered with black peat mud. Two bulls out on the rocks were facing up to each other, too busy with their own quarrel to bother with us; our arrival had probably driven them into each other's territories.

Angus went back to the dinghy and we soon heard his whistle. We ran back and found the dinghy awash and broadside on; so off they went, to be back in a week's time.

I started carting my gear to the slope of the east hill, clear of seal ground but in full view of the beach. I chose a patch of strong brown mat grass, to get a bit of upholstery under the tent. Seals were beginning to land again as I pitched the tent. I was all set and snug by dusk, with geese flying noisily overhead and the ululations of seals coming on the breeze. A wet smacking noise made me look out; there were two big bulls, one in a pool on the rocks, the other on the edge, propped up like a sealion and slapping its side with a flipper. In the last of the light I could see hunching forms moving about. At high water the surge and surf sounded loud from the outer darkness. I had candle and Primus and did well enough. Instead of frost, it rained hard all night.

The British Isles are now the world headquarters of the Atlantic grey seal, *Halichoerus grypus*; so it is surprising that it took such a long time for the elementary facts of the animals' life history to be recognized. Wild weather and the inaccessibility of the colonies are partly accountable; then for centuries human intervention was local and confined to hunting and harrying, and when early naturalists and sportsmen took an interest it was the usual story – their primary aim was to shoot trophies. Even in 1936 practically all the elementary facts in Edmund Sandars' delightful *Beast Book* were wildly wrong. Much more was known of the biology of Antarctic seals than of those of Britain.

27

In the early autumn the bulls in their prime haul ashore at the breeding grounds and establish territories. The heavily gravid cows follow and settle where they will to drop their thirty pound pups. For about a fortnight the cows suckle their young, on milk of extraordinary richness, then desert them, mate for next year's births, and go back to sea. So the cows are nearly always pregnant and the gestation period of almost a year is achieved by the embryo remaining in a state of suspended development for months on end, as also happens in some other seals and in a few other mammals, such as badgers. It seems that this intensive suckling followed by desertion was not well recognized until 1938 when Frank Fraser Darling went to North Rona for part of the seals' season. The pups gradually moult their baby coats, and at a month old are tight little barrels of blue-grey fur. They have to learn unassisted the seal's way of life. Apparently bulls and cows alike fast throughout their time ashore and at the end of it go back to sea skinny and spent.

Next day Shillay lay quiet under a grey sky. The crying of seal pups and the baa-ing of sheep came on the breeze, through the near noise of surf. After yesterday's disturbance the seals' own order was restored, and the sense was all of peace and possession. Yet this was the precarious time; evolution had not earned them full independence of land; necessity still drew them ashore to breed; the truncated suckling period, the unmotherliness of the dams, the hasty mating all contrived to shorten the dangerous time of parting from the comparative safety of the sea. Their whole hope of the future depended on these few vulnerable weeks.

Yet the littered pups slept like the dead. Some unhurried shuffling traffic moved up and down the beach. Cows slept or bickered amongst themselves with no more exertion than rolling over and waving a flipper; some lay flat on their backs, speckled bellies facing the sky. Bulls slept with one eye half open – no look outs posted, no anxious glances, none of the wariness so characteristic of wild animals in our world. Shillay belonged to the seals. Myself and tent were evidently no more to them than a boulder and that was pleasure enough.

I looked out and wondered what to make of all these stranded sea beasts – great aquatic dogs – legless bullocks – sea cows? Gaelic calls the grey seal *callach cuain* – ocean bear; to the French they are *veaux marins*. Common nomenclature is no help at all, being totally confused. Seals may be cattle-like yet they are carnivores through and through; but the adults are always bulls and cows, though they growl and snarl and even, according to Mrs Kennedy Fraser, collector of Gaelic songs, they sing. The young are pups, cubs or calves. The nouns of assembly are quaint and go back to the old days of sealing and whaling in ships under sail: a breeding colony is a rookery, and group of swimming seals is a pod.

The confusion is man made. Never mind the names, the animals live in their own right, competent and successful: supremely confident in the roughest seas, surely enjoying their mastery under water, unaware of cold yet basking in the sun's warmth, unembarrassed by their own awkwardness on land.

The seal herd on the beach showed all the colours of cross-bred cattle and seemed describable in the same terms – brindles and roans and dapples. Most handsome were a few mole-coloured bulls, great brutes with necks wreathed in folds of blubber, and coats sleek and bloomed even in dull light. At the sea's edge a bull took hold of one of his cows; he bit into the scruff of her neck, like a cockerel mounting a hen, and grasped her with his flippers. They struggled awhile in the surf, the bull showing his large red organ; when connection was made they settled and lay like flotsam in the sandy breakers, stomach to back in a close embrace. A white pup was caught in the backwash of a wave and drawn away. The mother near at hand took no notice but lay on her side ready to suckle. I thought the pup lost but it kept struggling back, only to be washed off again. In the end, with the tide ebbing, it was safe. The cow lay over on her side and the pup suckled. The bull ended his long embrace but was soon after another cow in the surf. A rival bull came humping up; first bull retreated, turning and snarling; cow made away to sea between the two.

I looked long enough from my camp of nearby boulders, thinking it best to keep well clear at first, then took a turn round the hill. Visibility eastwards was rain-washed clear as far as the Cuillins in Skye, fifty miles away. Coppay and Toe Head lay north-eastwards, then Gasker was sharp, twelve miles due north – another seal island and, like Shillay, with an offlying subsidiary rock. Beyond Gasker even the ultimate speck of the Flannan Isles was showing, nearly forty miles away.

Cliffs carry right round the north and west coasts of Shillay, indented here and there with slab-sided *geos*, miniature versions of fiords. A peregrine sprang out from the cliffs, a frieze of cormorants craned their necks from a ledge above the surge, a not-quite-right thrush among the rocks was a redwing, come from Scandinavia to winter in Shillay! A formation of four migrant swans took a momentary gleam of sunshine on their wings as they beat steadily towards the Sound. The main flock of sheep was grazing on the hillside – their attendant starlings rose in a cloud. One close-grazed slope of sedge and dwarfed heather was marked all over with big bird droppings – this was goose pasture. Over a squashy tract of buckshorn plantain littered with crab remains the gulls were protesting as it if were summer. I came on round and there in the west was St Kilda, faint and clear, and the black saddle-backed hump of Haskeir, eighteen miles away in the south-west: Gasker, Shillay, Haskeir, the three main seal nurseries of the Atlantic coast.

From the southern slope of the hill the rest of the island's simple topography lay plain – a peninsula cliffbound on the seaward side, low and rocky on the other, littered with boulders and marked with seal pools, the biggest of them a dirty little lake. From up here it was sometimes difficult to tell which were seal pups and which lumps of bleached driftwood – the observers on the Seal Flight had had the same trouble. The point of the peninsula is a rocky land's end, Ard an Laoigh, detached by a deep gully, partly sea floored and not negotiable by seals or sheep. Beyond is Little Shillay, isolated by a turbulent channel. The crown of the rock, half a mile from where I sat on the hill was peppered light and dark – it was solid with barnacle geese. The far end of the peninsula is rock faced until, coming back towards the hill, the rocks give way to the precious strip of beach with its backing of miniature sand cliff and dunes. 'Where there is sand there is hope' has long been my axiom in the Hebrides, for the context of black peat and wet rock is without hope. The near end of the sand is fenced by a whaleback of rock with a narrow passage through to a boulder beach on the other side. The mudslide of squashed turf and wallows and peaty pools rises from the boulders into the slope of the hill. From the boulder beach the coast hardens again into rock and then on northwards into cliff. I looked down on to my tiny tent standing a few yards in from the rock.

During a few days I could hardly expect to understand much of the seals' social arrangements, but some elementary patterns did emerge and I began to recognize individuals. I made friends – or at least I was friendly – with a rather scruffy brown bull who lay by the whaleback rock separating boulder beach from sand, and moved up and down with the tide. He claimed his territory even when it was covered with water. He allowed me to squat within two or three yards and managed to put up with camera and tripod. This was a warming difference from the stampede caused by an anchoring boat; I suppose the chaos and panic caused by occasional shepherds and shepherding was only too well remembered.

In fact I found little difficulty in getting close to the seals or in moving among them. I hated to see the whites of their eyes; it is the infallible sign of fear and is evident only too often in published photographs. The great thing was to keep low and move slowly, sit still as much as possible and not appear as a figure on the skyline. Keeping downwind seemed less important though the sense of smell must have been mutual – I kept getting wafts of the peculiar acrid smell of the colony. And the cows recognised their own pups by smell; often I watched

31

a cow moving among pups, sniffing at one muzzle after another, and snapping until she found the right one. When bulls were on the move the pups hastily shuffled out of the way as best they could. Unwary ones would be snapped up and flung aside in an explosion of irritability.

Census taking caused some unavoidable disturbance. I counted a grand total of 192 live pups, about equally divided between inland grass and wallows, and shoreside rocks and beaches. There were only five dead pups. This third week of October was evidently the height of the season for Shillay. By this time only a few pups were new born and very few had yet reached the sea. By contrast most of the pups on Gasker had been born by the end of September; these differing dates for the peak of pupping has since become, with increasing observation, one of the arguments for supposing the various seal islands to be closed communities. However far the pups and yearlings may wander – and tagging has shown that it can be hundreds of miles – they are supposed to return at maturity to the island of their birth.

Peak of the season it was, yet action seemed incidental against the overall impression of slumber. The real and intense activity was hidden and inward. In two or three weeks the pups treble their weight, from thirty pounds at birth to some ninety pounds at weaning. The cows slowly shrink like a pricked balloon, the pups swell in exchange. The soft white baby coat of the pups must serve as insulation until blubber takes over. Among all young animals the newborn pups are as irresistible as any. Their coats are far too big for them. I picked up a hand—an oversized glove with nothing inside; the wide black eyes looked up mute and myopic. A little older and sometimes the eyes streamed with tears. It has not saved them from clubbing.

In all the island the only human artefact, apart from a fragment of dry stone wall in the dunes, was the sheep fank, a gaunt enclosure of driftwood and wire erected at the head of a gully in the rocks. White pups lay in and around it. In quiet weather a boat could lie against a natural jetty in the gully.

The only sign of human life during my stay was a small

boat I saw below when I was up the hill. I thought it was lay-ing lobster creels along the coast but it headed close in and stopped: a Berneray boat, *Speedwell*, CY 169. I went to the rocks and just within shouting range heard the faint words 'thought you were wrecked'. I shouted back that I was there on purpose. Years afterwards when I had come to know the crew (and the *Heather* used to borrow their mooring in Bays Loch, Berneray) I heard the fable they had told themselves. An aeroplane had gone very low over Berneray in the night – I heard it too over Shillay. Next morning on the way out to the lobster grounds they had spotted a new white mark on the island. So the aeroplane had crashed on Shillay: my tent was the remains of it. And when they saw the mannie coming down the hill they said, 'Well, there's one survivor anyway'.

One early morning the tent was slatting as usual but something was different – the sun! I bundled out and there was the round red sun rising over the Harris hills. All day the island lay in a flood of sunshine. Next day was the same, and the next; it was benison; the breeze died away and as the short days ended the wet sand turned pink, the seals became black slugs, and a sickle moon rode over Pabbay.

I spent much time keeping company with the scruffy brown bull, admiring his roman profile and looking into his rheumy eye. When he lay slumbering on his side an occasional wheezy sigh came forth; he indulged in luxurious full length stretches from muzzle to quivering tail stump; he could hunch himself a yard or two on his side without bothering to roll over. But a watchful eye opened now and then in case of trespassers. His days were enlivened by fighting and copulation.

Bull fights were real and red. The whole seal ground was an invisibly marked-out chessboard where a bull's move usually met check. Most of the trouble seemed to arise when bulls were trying to get out of the sea or back into it. A couple of bulls faced up to each other, growling horribly, mouths wide open. If one did not give way, they closed, tearing at each other's necks. The great bodies thumped on the sand or threshed in the surf, sending spray flying; 'a bloody conflict',

33

said Martin, 'which gives a red tincture to the sea in that part where they fight . . .' and so I saw it too. When a desperate bout ended and one or the other broke away, the churned-up sand was blood stained. The brown bull had open wounds on neck and back, and a gash under one eye, but he seemed indifferent. When he floated off, coupled with one of his cows from the boulder beach, the waves banged them down on the stones, but it might have been a feather bed. Often a pair drifted offshore, and sank, the two heads only showing occasionally; the couplings could last half an hour.

One of the boulder beach cows was a particularly tolerant creature, who let me sit beside her. She lay like a bolster dumped among the boulders, her chin resting on cold wet stone, like a dog on the hearth, her whiskers silvery in the sunshine. Sometimes she turned to sniff the pup alongside her, and the pup sometimes broke his sleep for the only sign of baby playfulness he revealed – he rolled on his back and bit his nails and waved his hands in the air. A couple of hours of pale autumn sunshine was enough to parch the mother. With many backward looks to her pup she went down to the sea, stopped to drink at a rock pool, then glided deep into green water. She went away dry and fawn coloured and came back a sleek grey.

I knew one moulted pup at the beginning of his travels. He left a heap of moulted fur on the mudslide and moved down to the shore. There he lay among the rocks and spent most of his time chewing a stick of laminaria. All the pups lay separately. I never saw one greet another and motherly attention was confined to muzzle sniffing and suckling; it seemed a sad and lonely babyhood, made more so by the tears and crying.

The mudslide above the boulder beach was a good place to watch, for it was one end of the seal ground and the downwind end in any westerly air. I could squat by a boulder and watch from outside without intrusion. Some pups slept upside down in the dirty pools with their heads under water. Evidently the adult capacity for long submersion was developed at an early age. When they hauled out the matted fur soon dried out to toy-like fluff. Here on the mudslide the chessboard pattern was at its clearest, where each bull lay among his harem of up to half a dozen cows, within an area of a few square yards. Here I soon recognized the cow's characteristic repulse to a bull's advances. She stretched up her neck, wreathing and snapping at his face, meanwhile hooting and moaning with open mouth; and the free flipper whirred. A cow's flipper was full of expression. When she lay on her side and the pup was seeking the extruded nipple the flipper would irritably signal him aft – further back, further back. 'There is a hole in the skin of the female,' said Martin, 'within which the teats are secured from being hurt as it creeps along the rocks and stones . . .' The hooting and moaning of the cows made the ululation that carried on the breeze after dark, Gaeldom's song of the seals. Bulls merely snarl or hiss.

Even the massive bulls managed the slippery uphill climb of the mudslide without difficulty, progressing like enormous looper caterpillars, with a muscular ripple passing along their bellies. They reversed in the same way, when driven back by a cow or another bull. They only used their claws on rough rock. And they showed a surprising turn of speed, as when a bloody-headed bull ran the gauntlet of the beach to get to the sea. Then the flippers dug in hard, leaving a double track of claw marks in the sand, and the body went along with such resounding thumps it seemed to be as much off the ground as on it. When I was laced up at night in my sleeping bag I felt like a seal myself.

Landing would have been possible during most of my time on Shillay, but the appointed day for the *Bluebell*'s return was like summer. In the warm afternoon sunshine I sat on a boulder and watched the blue speck approaching. We went rolling home over the deep blue sea in a world lying in windless peace. There had been a touch of frost in the morning, Murdo said, hoar frost on the boat. In the evening the mainland shore was so quiet, no sound but the gurgling of the tide, and the moon laid a track across the water. The last few days on Shillay seemed an idyll, I had forgotten the long frustrating wait beforehand and the lashing wind and rain.

Everyday life, the newspapers and the advertisements, were dreary enough after the island world of seals. I knew I must go back another time for a proper stay. I wanted to join in, to follow individual pups through from birth to weaning and moulting and going to sea. I wanted to see what it would be like to live alone on the island for a month or more; or rather, since it was a Scottish island, to see 'what like it would be'.

# THREE

◆

# *Gasker and Pabbay*

On a fair summer day in July 1949, we sailed for Gasker in the *Heather*. There is no sort of anchorage at the islet, its coast is rockbound, the water is deep even close in, and the bottom is rock. The ever-helpful Murdo had come along to look after the boat assisted by Leslie Lomas and his younger son Michael from Kyles Lodge, while the crew, John Naish, Brian Roberts and myself could get ashore. Dr B. B. Roberts was the polar expert at the Foreign Office and also worked at the Scott Polar Research Institute, Cambridge. This was his first trip in the *Heather* and the purpose of the voyage, as ever, was to reach and explore uninhabited islands. In later years we became the basic and often the sole crew.

The dripping wet sea fog of the morning had cleared to cloudless sunshine. Murdo piloted us close along the Harris shore over Mediterranean sea colours, translucent green over sand, deep dense blue over rock and weed, and the swell broke snowy white at the rocks. We passed the marvellous sands of Northton, enclosed at the far end by Rudh an Team-puill, where the little ruined temple stood in silhouette on a rocky knoll. Once again Toe Head opened beyond Bretasker and 'vessels can steer out to sea'; the horizon was sharp as a razor. But the brilliant day soon clouded over. Taransay drew slowly past inshore and then Murdo's infamous Glorigs, marked by a welter of broken water. Gasker ahead was a bright green mound with a rim of black rock.

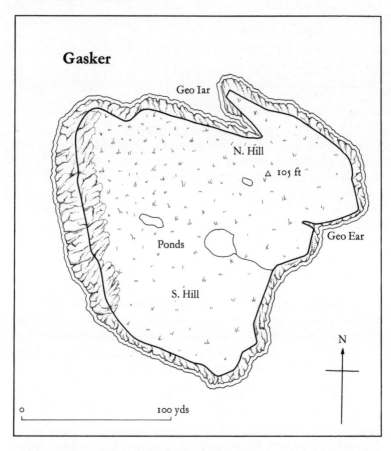

We passed the bare skerry of Gasker Beg and nosed in cautiously to the eastern side, took a turn up and down and stopped to launch the dinghy. We rowed in and made a poor choice of a landing place. However, we got ashore, dragged up the dinghy without damage, and climbed inland to explore.

It was a strange place. At once we were walking over hard dry peat. The Outer Isles had been dried off in a rare drought and some of the heather was burnt brown. Here on Gasker the bare peat was crazed with deep fissures like the bottom of a dried-up pond. The islet was black and green, a garden of flowers, a lush meadow, against black rock and bare peat. In spite of the exposure the air was heavy with the cloying sweet smell of scurvy grass and sea campion.

On any sufficiently remote islet there is always the hope of finding an unknown colony of Leach's petrels. We have got to go to the last fringes of land to meet seals and petrels: seals come in to mainland beaches only for the want of offshore islands but to the small dusky petrels mainland is untouchable, as alien and hostile as the ocean to a naked man. Land must be a small island but only remote isles will serve; even then they will come ashore only under cover of darkness and disappear underground. In all their lives only a rare individual can ever meet a human being, except in the guise of a ship. For storm petrels inshore islands are acceptable but Leach's petrels choose only the farthest and fewest dots in the ocean. Gasker, for all its loneliness, was probably much too landward for them. It is only five and a half miles from the nearest point of mainland Harris; but it was worth a search.

Here on the island, between inland peat and shoreside rock, there were some small but useful-looking areas of dry, loose boulders. We started sniffing round the stones and soon got the characteristic whiff of petrel in several places. We had a borrowed pick and a spade and set to work. Most of the boulders were immovable but after working away beneath a big one I reached in and touched a feather. More work and I could see an egg and then the petrel squatting beyond it. Excavation from the other side drove it into my hand – a pretty little storm petrel. When I let it go it zig-zagged fast and low over the ground and away to sea; the gulls took no notice. Later on we got another one from a different place, but the auspices were not favourable. Stormies always have a predilection for loose dry stones but Leach's petrels prefer some earth and turf to work in; the Gasker peat was quite unmarked by bird burrows, and anyway it must be too wet for most of the year.

Gasker was not much of a bird island. Fulmars had not colonized; the cliffs were relatively insignificant, though white-washed in places; the boulders sheltered a very few puffins. But there was a breeding colony of arctic terns and a flock of turnstones some fifty strong. The usual gulls protested overhead – herring, great and lesser black-backs, and also two or three pairs of common gulls. Eider families were swimming offshore, they had left behind plenty of used nests. Gasker was evidently much more a seal than a bird metropolis.

The whole island is only some fifty acres in extent and more or less round, with a modest summit only 105 feet high. This hill rises at the north end and falls southward to a saddle across the island, marked by two big ponds. Beyond them a lesser hill, a low mound of peat, makes up the rest of the inland. The pair of ponds, each fifty or sixty yards across, was the feature of the island and the evident centre of the seal colony. A stony gully with a trickle of water led down from the lower pond to the rocks, and provided the seals' obvious main highway to and from the sea. The water levels had subsided and uncovered muddy stony shores, which toad rush was fast colonizing. All around were pools and slides and peat hags with black walls a yard high, and all about lay the bones and skeletons of seals. It was like the remains of a fair, everyone had gone away and nothing was left but the litter. In the autumn all this area must be a nearly continuous seal wallow and the peat of the southern mound a black morass. Now the peat was dry and the seals long gone, greenstuff burgeoned in a brave attempt to cover the scars of winter. Tussocks of sea-pink had survived the churning though most of the plants overwintered as seeds. Here were the pretty mauve flowers of sea spurrey and the pretty pink of sea milkwort, but mayweed was the chief mantle, strong clumps covered with daisy flowers. Silverweed reached out bright red runners almost visibly growing; lush chickweed and scurvy grass, orache and sorrel squashed juicily underfoot, all running free as long as the summer should last.

The loneliness of a new-born pup

Atlantic Grey Seal. Growth of a male pup from 1st to 20th day. All photos are to the same scale.

a   1st day – muzzle pre-natally moulted

b   3rd day – moult continuing on muzzle, umbilical cord still visible

c   7th day – front edges of fore paws begin to moult

d   13th day – weaned about now

e   17th day – moult more than half complete

f   20th day – moult practically complete

Hostile reaction of a very young pup

The north hill stays green in winter, for Gasker, Gas-sker, named by the Norsemen, means goose skerry and is famous grazing for migrant flocks of barnacle geese.

Martin said of the island: 'it excels any other plot of its extent, for fruitfulness in Grass and Product of Milk, it maintains 8 or 10 Cows; the Natives kill seals here which are very big'. On our day a flock of twenty sheep was in residence but they had not managed to make any impression on the vegetation; they walked in a hayfield of flowering grasses. The north hill was given over to plantains, in parts a close sward of buckshorn plantain, where I found a solitary frog orchid, in others a meadow of ribwort and sea plantain. The flank of the hill grew such dense beds of devilsbit scabious that they looked as if planted – a crop of cos lettuces. I never saw lesser celandines like these, so far removed from the enamelled petals of March sunshine; here the gross plants rambled like creepers among the boulders and the last few flowers were pale and shut. Martin's fruitfulness was well understood; the massive manuring by geese and gulls and the waste of seals was sufficient explanation. I was busy stuffing greenery into a camera case, making a customary collection for the Natural History Museum, in the usual haste of an island landing, with one eye on the weather and the other on the waiting boat. I collected forty-two species and no doubt more could be added at leisure.

Dr J. A. Harvie-Brown, the celebrated naturalist and yachtsman, visited Gasker in 1887 for an hour. A year later he published his *Vertebrate Fauna of the Outer Hebrides.** His choice of landing places was better than ours. Two deep geos cut into the cliffs at the north end, Geo Ear facing east and the bigger Geo Iar facing north-west. The big one was remarkably calm inside in spite of the south-westerly swell and was accessible down to sea level by a series of terraces on one side, but a boat would have to be hauled up vertically.

* *Vertebrate Fauna of the Outer Hebrides* by Dr J. A. Harvie-Brown (David Douglas, Edinburgh, 1888)

Geo Ear looked better, well sheltered, and with rock walls less steep and more broken into steps. Harvie-Brown used both.

We kept an eye on the *Heather* dodging to and fro off shore. After about three hours someone was waving, evidently they didn't like the look of the weather. St Kilda and the Flannans were sharp enough to seaward but mist was rolling out from the mainland and the breeze was freshening. John rowed the dinghy round into Geo Ear and we got off easily.

Gasker is half the size of Shillay but the seal colony is much bigger; though only five miles off Scarp on the Harris coast it is more remote than Shillay and wholly Atlantic. 'On the rock of Gasker', (wrote William MacGillivray in his *A History of British Quadrupeds*, 1838) 'twelve miles from Harris, in the Atlantic, it [the grey seal] is found on shore in great numbers, along with its young . . . and so many as a hundred and twenty seals have been killed there in one day'. The year before the Seal Flight of 1947 and of my week on Shillay, the Fishery Cruiser *Rona* had happened to be on the west side, and visited Gasker. By a strange coincidence a boat's crew from Harris had chosen the same day and were caught in the act of clubbing young seals. The instant retribution must have seemed like divine intervention; it was talked of for years afterwards. On that day the ship's officers estimated the total population as about a thousand animals and the veteran Scottish naturalist, Seton Gordon, who was on board, reckoned there were five hundred pups. The ship came back again in subsequent years; on 6 November, 1950, the estimate was seven to eight hundred pups and Seton Gordon who was again on board recorded 'upwards of a hundred' seal pups lying dead – a catastrophe which has never been explained, except that the greater the density of seal pups in a colony, the greater is the mortality. There were four to five hundred pups the following year. In summer only a few seals live round the island – about twenty-five heads in the surf on our day. Gasker has turned out to be a major colony, second only to the seals' famous British headquarters on far away Rona.

The shepherd of Pabbay, Lachie Macleod, 'a very wild man', was a famous character in the district.

Pabbay is a big beautiful empty island of sand and short grass, two miles across, the first island inwards from Shillay. The census of 1841 returned a population of 338 but all the people were cleared soon afterwards and had to emigrate to Australia and Canada. In 1961 the population was two. Since then the island has been uninhabited for most of the year, but the census of 1971 happened to coincide with the lambing season and there were four inhabitants. The enumerator, Miss Paterson, made a special voyage to count them.

Pabbay is two faced, like Shillay. The gentle side of white sand beaches and dunes looks to Berneray and the Sound, the wild side of rock walls lies open to the Atlantic. All the wide grassy slopes of the interior rise and gather into the pyramidal central hill, the welcome seamark of Beinn à Charnain.

We first landed on Pabbay early on a July morning, in flat calm: no sign of life, no sound from inland but the crowing of a rooster. The short dewy turf was fragrant with bedstraw. A bunch of stags moved magnificently away from the low ground, unhurriedly leapt a stone wall, and stopped to look back.

We were investigating the ruins of the village when we saw the man. He came with a slow stride down the hill, staff in hand, dog at heel, telescope slung across his back.

The figure turned out to be no dour Gael but a friendly, merry man, happy-go-lucky and careless of the days. He soon had us in the house for tea and home-baked scone bread. Macleod had been ten years shepherding in Patagonia and the Falklands, and sometimes wished he'd never come home. Now he had been three years in Pabbay, usually alone. Provisions came out once a month from Rodel but he liked to grow his own potatoes; the longest time without a visit had been for two weather-beaten winter months. Water had to be fetched in buckets from the burn up the hill, a longish walk. At present he had a mate with him, a Macdonald from Harris. They lived in a low stone cottage with two chimneys, thatched, lined with match boarding, barely furnished, and damp. A calendar above the mantelpiece was crossed off day by day; today, 9 July 1949, had already been cancelled.

The livestock on the island was five hundred sheep, sixty cattle and some calves, two horses, two dogs, some hens, twenty red deer stags and forty hinds. The men had a tame yearling hind, which stood on its hind legs and boxed with them. It hung about outside the house and kept company with a tame sheep. A year later, so I was told in Rodel, the hind still followed them up the hill like a dog 'and of course if they sit down, she takes a rest too'.

The Pabbay deer were introduced in the 1880's by the then proprietor and they flourished but now, said Macleod, they no longer breed properly, the stock was too inbred. Sometimes a gentleman came to shoot them; sportsmen's quarters was a corrugated iron hut by the cottage.

In the old days Pabbay was famous for its barley, supposed to be the best grown anywhere in the Outer Isles, and the natives were famous for their illicit distilling. The exciseman was forever trying to catch them. Macdonald had a family story about it. One of his forefathers was a Pabbay man, though he lived in Harris; his was the only boat that would take the exciseman, and whenever he would bring the exciseman to Pabbay he would be hoisting a brown sail with a white patch, for a signal. Until one day the sail was torn and he did not know what to do at all; so he started off and when he got near the shore he ran the boat onto a rock and he shouted at the pitch of his voice, 'Help, help, come and save the chentleman, the exciseman!'

In winter Pabbay was ringed with lobster creels. Once, said Macleod, he had a dog which wanted off, he was pining for the mainland and he would be waiting on the rocks by the shore. A passing lobster boat from Berneray saw this anxious dog, and thought the worst. The crew landed and went to the house. There was no one in the room, the fire was out. They were feared to look in the bedroom. One said, 'you look', and the other said, 'you look', they were afraid of what they would find, and they went away without looking. They went and told Campbell, shopkeeper of Rodel and owner of the island, and he sent them back. Next day they saw Macleod walking on the shore. He had been away up the hill.

Another time, said Macleod, when he landed in Harris he was asked if his leg was better. It was known that he'd hurt his leg in the island. Someone in Berneray had happened to train a telescope on Pabbay, at more than three miles range, and had seen him limping down the hill; and so the story got round. But Macleod had only fallen asleep on the hill, and woke up with pins and needles and started off limping. 'The earth is the best of beds', he said.

The sun was hot. We bathed in the green water – but as momentarily as ever in the Hebrides – and lay on the turf and talked long with Macleod. I liked to hear of Macleod's solitary arrangements; he preferred to be alone and as it appeared was looking for a way to regain his former solitude. He had a wireless set but only had it on for an hour in the evening, listening to the BBC's European service; it was odd to hear him speak of *Pravda* and his speech was sprinkled with out-of-date RAF slang. He left Pabbay only once a year, for a fortnight's holiday which he spent drinking. 'You get ashore, and well, when you're over wiz the first hit, it's time to go back again.' But two years later, when we next called at Pabbay, it was Macleod who had left, and Macdonald, joined by a brother, who had stayed.

A peculiarity of Pabbay is the smooth white pebbles to be found in places on the shore. When two are rubbed together in darkness they glow with a pale light and give off a smell of gunpowder. Martin missed this particular phenomenon, though it was just the sort of thing he liked to note, but he did report the wooden harbour, so called 'because the sands at low water discover several trees that have formerly grown

45

there. Sir Norman Macleod told me that he had seen a tree cut there, which was afterwards made into a harrow'. At that time the steward of St Kilda lived in Pabbay; now a St Kilda toy mailboat, once washed up, was preserved in the cottage.

Since the island has lain empty the sands have crept inland. They devoured the big lagoon, marked on the first Admiralty chart of 1857 but now long lost under continuous sand dunes; all that remains is a little freshwater pool to receive the hillside burn. Sand has heaped up against the walls of the old inland village; some of the sandbanks were permanently fixed under short turf, some were still being bound by marram grass. Along the shore lyme grass grew stiff and straight like a field near to harvest. The peninsula of Quinish, a bar of rock, sand and shingle, accessible at low water, was occupied by a noisy concourse of common and arctic terns. Their closely packed nests were substantial pads made of lyme grass leaves. Little terns laid their two eggs straight into a scoop in the bare sand. Ringed plovers and dunlins twinkled along the shore. The grass of ungrazed islets on the bar sank underfoot like a cushion; eiders and common gulls nested on them.

Two years later we visited Pabbay again. This time Macleod was back and alone, and the *Heather*'s crew was only Brian Roberts and myself. He was as easily cheerful as before, letting the world go by. He had been away for a couple of years as an estate handyman and ostensibly had left Pabbay because of the housing but the real reason was the denial of his solitude. Now the old cottage was partly demolished, serving as a quarry for the new half-built cottage nearby. The stone gable ends were up, and the timber framing and asbestos sheets between them, but work had long been held up for want of labour. Macleod was living in the corrugated iron hut, neat and clean within; he remarked on the two pitfalls of solitary living, the extremes of fanatical tidiness one way or of complete fecklessness the other.

In the evenings he went in for rug making, for competitions, working to his own designs and using Harris wool. He made the predictable comment, so often heard on the fringes of habitation: 'It passes the time.' He had made a bowl for carrying hen food by cutting an aluminium net float in half with a stump of hacksaw blade; it had taken two or three evenings. There were only two hens and only one was laying. He asked for books, so afterwards I sent a load from home.

Macleod had second sight, as was proper to his solitary state; he told of two instances, visions of deaths which came to pass, but it was 'kind of intimate'. He did not care for priests, an attitude hardened by his days in Patagonia; he was contemptuous of local narrow-mindedness and hypocrisy and was always ready for religious battles in the bar. It amused him that two of his stories were of the sort to be heard from a pulpit. The Lord will provide: once he and Macdonald were short of food; he'd shot a duck; he told Macdonald it would be good if they could get onions and potatoes to go with it; he went down to the beach and found onions and a turnip washed up. When they were out of bread and had no baking powder or soda he said to Macdonald, 'you'll get your fresh bread', and he found a tin of yeast unspoilt, lying in the high water wrack.

He came on board for drinks and supper, and we went back with him to the hut. He set off in the dusk with a bucket, in search of the cow, and came back to make tea and flapjacks. We left him late at night and never saw him again.

But four years later we only missed him by a month. He had left Pabbay and gone south to work at the rocket range; two lads from Harris had moved into the new cottage the day before us but were to stay for only a month or two.

I walked up the hill for an aerial view down to Shillay on the other side, while Brian went to collect more of the special pebbles. On the summit stood a brand new Ordnance Survey cairn, enclosed by a stone wall. The primary triangulation of Britain was being re-surveyed; on island summits we kept coming across the surveyors' works and more than once caught up with the parties themselves. Shillay lay map-like below, with its bright strip of sand and well remembered features – the only island I have thought of as 'mine', the only one I have ever lived on alone. I came down the western fall of the hill, by rocks where mountain everlasting spread in close mats, and past the two shallow stony lochans, Heddal More and Beg, now pretty with water lobelia.

The days of proper habitation on Pabbay, even by ones and twos, were now ending. Altogether Macleod's reign had spanned eleven years. He was last heard of in Skye; there was some sort of accident; perhaps he had been knocked over on the road by a car and had managed to get home; he was found dead in his shepherd's cottage.

# FOUR

## *Haskeir and Causamul, Monach and Deasker*

One of the axioms of Hebridean cruises in the *Heather* was: In settled weather get out on the west side. Sooner or later in the course of years hot sunshine and a marvellous calm will spread over the western ocean. On one such day we came out from West Loch Roag, where we had been storm bound for ten days, and headed southwards down the Atlantic coast of the Outer Isles. We even stopped to bathe over the side; the engine room, instead of offering its usual welcome of smelly warmth, was for once far too hot; we went naked on deck.

We stopped overnight in Loch Tamanavay and came on next day by the Sound of Scarp, inside Taransay, and back to Leverburgh for fuel. The weather held. Here at last was a chance to try for Haskeir, the big black sea rock eight miles off the coast of North Uist: Haskeir of the seals and seabirds, the refuge which Martin failed to reach on his voyage to St Kilda in 1697, the staging point which the Reverend Kenneth Macaulay used on his voyage of 1758.

We passed inside Shillay, the empty beach staring white under the summer sun, the mudslide now showing as a bright green stripe, the lowlands dotted only with boulders. We set a compass course for Haskeir; there was nothing to be seen in the seaward haze though the sun was as hot as ever and the water glassy.

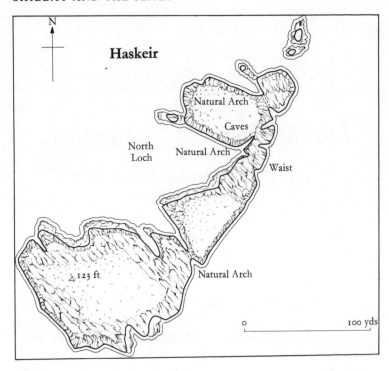

Haskeir began as a monotone lump against the light but soon the silhouette resolved into sharp crags, tusks and overhangs; two sea tunnels opened up, cutting clean through the rock like a couple of windows. We got close up to the rock walls and cruised up and down. A few seals slid into the water; the place was alive with all the stir of a seabird rock, the circling auks and fulmars, the whitened ledges, the rows of shags flopping down into the water, the rafts of birds floating offshore. There seemed to be several easy-looking places for landing along the east side.

Another *Heather* axiom was: Anchor only in sight of the bottom – but there was no hope of that here. The chart marked a five fathom patch; we sounded to and fro but couldn't find it. The best we got was a touch of the bottom at twenty fathoms, the full length of our anchor cable. We lay stopped in a state of indecision, the boat riding gently on the swell, the black wall of Haskeir close at hand; if we don't land now we never shall. There is always something fearful or ominous about being out in the ocean and up against a great rock. We were three of a crew – John Naish as usual, Christopher Harley, my erstwhile first lieutenant in wartime Coastal Force craft, and myself – so one of us could have stayed on board, but in all the years of the *Heather* and of her varying crews no one but me would ever take any interest in the engine and only I had the knack of starting it, crouching doubled-up at the starting handle and swinging it over against compression without actually suffering a rupture.

Then we found bottom a little closer in, at seventeen fathoms, and decided to try anchoring at that. The anchor found bottom and momentarily snagged with still a little cable to spare. We let the rest of it go, and so it did; the end of the cable appeared through the hawse pipe and flipped over the side – gone. Whoever had stowed the cable on board had omitted to shackle the end to the ring bolt down in the chain locker. It was not our fault but that was not much consolation with anchor and twenty fathoms of heavy chain cable now lying for evermore at the bottom of the sea.

That being that, we took a turn round the rock, cut between it and Haskeir Eagach – the row of detached black teeth to southward – and went sadly on our way.

But there was another chance a few years later, though when it came we made it even more difficult; Brian Roberts and I wanted to be on the rock at night. In 1939 R. B. Freeman, ornithologist, had reported a first finding of a single Leach's petrel in a hole on Haskeir; there might be a colony and the only sure way of finding out was to be there at night when the birds, if any, would be noisily and unmistakably flying about. We should have to charter a boat, so we went to see the genial John Angus Patterson, the Berneray ferryman, later to become famous as pilot for royal fishing trips in the Sound of Harris. His big decked launch, the *Dunbeath Castle*, had never had a coat of varnish since the day he'd bought her and the Kelvin Ricardo engine sounded as if it had never had a drop of oil. Once he cheerfully told me his motto for navigation among the rocks and shoals of the Sound: 'one bump and she's over'. I since wondered whether he bore this in mind when piloting the royal barge.

At the time we were lying in Bays Loch, Berneray, on a borrowed mooring, as usual, and in nice quiet weather. We had made our arrangements with John Angus but in spite of sitting up with him until after midnight had been unable to get him to speak of money. He had never been to Haskeir but in his splendid outgoing way was ready to try anything.

Next morning the glass was rising sharply and the weather brightening; the forecast was of sunshine and a moderate breeze to give way to a depression coming in from the west. We were away at five in the afternoon, towing our own dinghy: out by the Sound of Berneray, then southward of Boreray, then due west for Haskeir. St Kilda and Haskeir came in sight together as we cleared Griminish Point, the promontory of North Uist. The pencil of the Monach Islands lighthouse stuck out from the sea to the southward, and nearer lay the low rocks of Causamul. The narrow round-bottomed launch went with a quick roll and a fast revving racket of engine, very different from the staid plod of the *Heather*. The breeze fell light, and Haskeir stood black at the head of the glittering sun track. We were banking on a few hours of calm before the depression arrived, and that was just what we got.

Haskeir is no more than a narrow strip of rock, exactly half a mile long, lying north-east and south-west, low in the middle and about a hundred feet high at either end. We arrived and as before cut through between Haskeir and Haskeir Eagach to take a preliminary turn round the island. The five stricken forms of Haskeir Eagach opened one after the other and stood apart, the bare crags dramatically lit by the lowering sun, fanged and tusked, a desperate group. The two elevated ends of Haskeir stick out westwards, making a sort of bay between them on the Atlantic side – 'North Loch' – now full of swell and surf; the twin crowns of the rock were green and stroked across by the flood of low sunlight. The two natural arches or sea tunnels through the rock opened and shut one after the other.

We rounded the northern end and cruised slowly down the east side, very close in, to choose a landing place. John Angus made nothing of the difficulties and I felt somewhat ashamed of our earlier timidity; but it is different with a crew to stay on board. He stopped the launch only a few yards out from the rock walls and threw the anchor over the side without ceremony.

We picked out a quiet looking place on the low lying central waist. It was near high water of a spring tide. John Angus backed in the dinghy – there was a swill and lift at the rocks but not enough to make difficulty – first one ashore, then the two rucksacks, then the other – and the dinghy rowed clear. It was half past eight, the sun still strong and warm and the air calm; we felt the small triumph of standing on a strange rock.

A few paces inland were enough to open the turbulent western bay. Here at its narrowest, and close under the cliffs of the northern hill, the waist separated two oceans; one way the rocks slid down to meet the swell and the spray hung as mist in the level sunlight, but on the other side the launch lay quietly with the men already dabbing fishing lines up and down over the side. In wintertime the swell would go over green from one side to the other. The cliff of the northern hill rose abruptly from the waist; it looked like an awkward passage. We left that for the time being and set off southwards to make the best of the evening sun. The waist soon broadened and began to rise into cliffs until it came to a sudden end at the main sea tunnel or natural arch. This turned out to be no more than a rocky hump-backed bridge. Within not much geological time it must collapse and then Haskeir will be two islands separated by a chasm. We passed a seal pool full of opaque water of a most virulent green and went on into the spacious southern block with its twin hills clothed in sea-pink. In early June passers-by have reported that Haskeir shows a beautiful rosy crown but now at the end of the month the sea-pink was already pale and going over.

Haskeir is a good strong seabird station, not a great one like the islands and stacs of St Kilda or Rona or Sula Sgeir, but a busy metropolis of ceaseless clamour and movement and smell. It is always the way at these rocky specks in the ocean; after the uniform eventless sea or the miles of hopeless peat hags they rise as sudden oases of life, caught up in the rush of their summer season.

A cloud of arctic terns rose from a rocky knoll and circled squawking above their scattered nests. John Angus saw them too and later on came off to get some eggs. Fulmars fluttered and pattered away, trying to get airborne from the meadows of sea-pink; some refused to budge and spat first oil, then vomit, according to customary routine. Here was the twentieth century mark of islands without man, when fulmars spread from the cliffs to nest on level ground. The nests were scrapes in the thrift hummocks or a few stone chips gathered together on rock ledges; the single eggs felt strangely cool after the hot clutches of other birds, reflecting the long drawn-out incubation of petrels. This summer evening was thirty-five years on from the days of the first fulmar settlers; now there were some five hundred nests. Haskeir could be summarized: sea-pink, fulmars and shags.

Shags made a frieze of craning necks along the rocks; they flapped heavily to and fro; they groaned from noisome caverns and came scrabbling out in their primordial unfinished way; the piled-up nests on the floor had each a heap of black and naked reptilian young and a surround of whitewash. Cliff ledges were lined with auks and any little knob served to support a kittiwake's nest; complaining gulls and oyster catchers added to the din; a few quiet eiders swam offshore.

The two modest hills of the southern crown are separated by a lower saddle with a dirty little lagoon. This was seal ground, the lagoon fringed with wallows now healed over by the press of summer growth. The fame of Haskeir has always been for seals but there was not much room for them. The area of wallows led down by rocky drains to the sea and to difficult landings; the central waist was easier but barred to

54

the south by the rock bridge; the whole northern hill was inaccessible.

The season of plants is as urgent in its way as the birds', but silent. Whatever grew on Haskeir and whatever chance seed arrived and survived was forced into rankness by dung and droppings, free from the discipline of grazing. Now the wallows grew a pure crop of sea plantain, nine inches deep. The thick maritime leaves squashed and crackled underfoot; the floor below the turgid canopy was bare black peat. Once some duck had dropped the seed of an American rush at the side of a little peat-bottomed pool; now the patch of *Juncus tenuis* was a yard across. Another bird had sown a seed of sea arrow grass, *Triglochin maritima*, beside the rushes, but so far it remained a single plant. Only twelve different plants – which was all I could find – had arrived at Haskeir. Two of them were grasses, but grass made no pasture, the red fescue and sea meadow grass grew only as tufts from rock clefts. The smell of fulmar wafted on the air, overpowering everything else; I had to go down on the ground to get the sweet smell of sea campion. Orache and mayweed sprawled at their rankest.

When our small adventure was over and done with, Haskeir was back in the distance, and I lay hot-eyed in my bunk, then in recollection the rock rose again to exert its powerful personality: stench and sweet smells, squalor and flowers, the angled rocks, the stir and clamour, the exposure of cliffs and ocean swell. Then the season runs out, the seals come and the birds go, and all that is left is a smear of rotting vegetation, bird-splashed rocks, sodden flattened nests, and an island washed over by rain and wind and spray.

We came back hot and thirsty to our cache by the landing place and rested in the last of the sun. Two centuries earlier the Reverend Kenneth Macaulay's evening on Haskeir must have been as idyllic as ours. He came to the rock in his six-oared highland boat for the crew to 'rest a little and divert themselves'. He was on his way to St Kilda, on 6 June, 1758. The day was quite sultry; he found the place extremely romantic, and stayed until ten o'clock in the evening. His crew made a great acquisition of wild fowl eggs 'unnecessary surely to men destined for St Kilda'. They told him how they caught the multitude of 'sea cormorants' (shags no doubt) in the caves; the method was abundantly simple, nor was the pastime at all disagreeable. 'A band of young fellows make a party, and after having provided themselves with a quantity of straw or heath, creep with great caution to the mouth of the cave which affords the game, armed with poles light enough to be easily wielded: this done, they set fire to the combustible stuff, and raise a universal shout; the cormorants, alarmed by the outcry, frightened by a glare so strange, and offended by the smoak, quit their beds and nests with the greatest precipitation, and fly directly towards the light: Here the sportsmen, if alert enough, will knock down a considerable number of them, and together with the cormorants, whole coveys of pigeons.'

The cliff leading up to the northern hill from the waist starts with an awkward overhang. Brian, being stout, called out to the launch to get a rope sent off. Once the overhang was done the rest was an easy staircase of ledges leading up to the crown; the green fall of land was dotted white with sitting fulmars. The sun was gone, sunk into a low bank of cloud along the horizon. We worked over the whole surface, crossed the narrow neck over the other sea tunnel and added a few token stones to a poor decrepit cairn. Another hump had a slab of rock humanly wedged upright into a cleft. Then we came on something more significant – the remains of a stone bothy built into the side of a rocky knoll, a little oblong enclosure with drystone walls still standing two or three feet high.

The most promising places for petrels seemed to be along the cliff edge above the bay. This was headquarters for the fifty-odd puffins, an area of loose boulders and clumps of sea-pink which met to make natural burrows below; but in burrows natural or excavated there was no sign of anything but puffin, and never a whiff of petrel. But clamour rose from the cliffs below and from the wall-sided cleft called East Liamp, where guillemots and kittiwakes whitened the ledges.

Razorbills occupied the smaller clefts, shags grunted from their stinking caverns; only the fulmars flew in silence, beat and glide, beat and glide, as inscrutable as ever.

At midnight we were back at the rucksacks for supper. An eider duck came and sat down nearby. St Kilda and Boreray still showed clear, with a sickle moon riding above them. And the other way the boatmen still dabbed their lines up and down, with now and then a gleam as another fish came in. They caught a load of small saithe and lythe, a few mackerel and even a couple of herrings. We went off again on another patrol, over the rock bridge to the south end – the route was getting familiar. Now colour was gone, all but a strip of orange in the north-west. The flying gulls, always in company, were black silhouettes but the terns poised overhead were beautiful, dimly lit from below by the horizon glow. Boot nails struck sparks from the rock. I remember the papery rustle of sea-pink as we walked and the brittle squash of dew-drenched plantains underfoot. Down at the south-east corner, below a stagnant rock pool, the big colony of fulmars kept cackling on their ledges; nothing else. We hung about the summit cairn while an area of loose stones nearby remained silent.

At half past one the night was as dark as it was going to be, a thick dusk. I went back alone to quarter the northern hill. The sea-pink flowers glimmered white as daisies on a lawn. Fulmars coughed and spat, seeing me first. I shone a torch down puffin burrows and got a glimpse of orange webbed foot or black wing. It was all just like my old pre-war island days, except that there were no petrels. The twittering of a nestful of young shags carried for more than fifty yards; no petrel could have been missed. A breeze began to stir and cloud was spreading up from the south. Still the bright horizon band in the north showed where the sun was travelling, and far off hills stretched in a black panorama from Scarp and Harris all the way round to Hecla and Beinn Mhor in South Uist.

At half past two the light was already coming back and colour returning; the daisy flowers of mayweed had yellow

57

centres again and the various leaves separated into different greens. By now the breeze was moderate and a lop and chop showed to seaward. It was time to go. We went once more to the south end, a familiar walk after six hours ashore, and lingered by the cairn, and looked back to the black cliffs.

At three o'clock we called out to John Angus that we were ready to come off. It was now dead low water and we chose a straight rock face. And it was time enough with the sea beginning to smack and splash in the new breeze. We got off with nothing worse than wet feet and backsides and a pocketful of water.

We watched an angry red dawn spread from the north-east; the first cloudlets were rosy from below but soon the dirty grey pall overtook us from behind, and the boat's exhaust was blowing out ahead. Our timing could not have been closer. We lay down in the cosy warmth alongside the engine and in that appalling racket actually managed to sleep for an hour. At six o'clock, when John Angus put us back aboard the *Heather*, Bays Loch was all on the run with a grey and white sea setting straight in. We waited an hour for the flood tide to make enough depth in the channel over the Reef, got a stove going and made some cocoa. When we sailed the *Heather* was punching even within the loch; we just scraped over the bar and headed across the Sound. How slow she seemed, after the rackety launch, just ambling and rolling along, unable to be hurried. By time we were back at the Harris shore and anchored in the Leverburgh boat pool, the day had declared itself in full: sheets of blowing rain and a gusting, moaning wind. And so to bed.

Boats from Berneray, Harris and Griminish, North Uist still go lobstering to Haskeir in the early summer, but the crews never go ashore. The old days were different. Towards the end of the nineteenth century boats used to be rowed out to the rock from Berneray, laden with creels and peats and oatmeal, and carrying fire. They landed and stayed as long as the weather allowed. In those days steamer and rail services were as comprehensive as now, or more so, providing a transport to market which contrasts oddly with the primitive state of the fishery.

About this time a boat's crew from Strond, in Harris, was caught at Haskeir and had to run before the gale. They ended up far out of sight of land, lost and exhausted. Then a shift of wind took them in to Gallon Head in Lewis. The one man still conscious managed to put the boat ashore on to a shingle beach – the boat was half full of water with the rest of the crew swilling helplessly in it. Local men saved them, and it was long enough before they were fit to go home.

But once, for a season, Haskeir had an inhabitant more substantial than occasional fishermen camping ashore; it was the tinker. I often asked after the tinker of Haskeir – some folklore or legend might remain in Uist or Berneray – I wrote to the *Stornoway Gazette* – but all without result. The year of the tinker seems to have been about 1830 and the only record of him, as far as I know, exists in a note in Erskine Beveridge's great work on North Uist.* 'It seems,' he wrote, 'that one autumn about eighty years ago, a tinker, "desiring to exercise some self-restraint", laid in a stock of provisions as also of materials for his trade, and sailed with these to the northern Haskeir. There he was left for a whole winter, having arranged with the boatmen to return for him early in the following year. Distinct traces of a rude stone hut may still be seen, not far from a small spring of fresh water, so that the general conditions fully agree with this account, even if it be hard to imagine how any one could choose such winter quarters, and very certain that the experiment was never repeated.'

I like to think that it was the tinker himself, rather than any fishermen, who built the bothy. Fishermen would want to be close to the boats and landing place; some rough sailcloth shelter or cave would have been their obvious quarters ashore. But the bothy is difficult of access and as high up as possible to escape at least some of the winter spray, yet

---

* *North Uist: its archaeology and topography with notes upon the early history of the Outer Hebrides* by Erskine Beveridge (Edinburgh, 1911)

tolerably sheltered by the knoll above. It must surely have been the tinker's home. In his winter season the tinker must have been isolated on the northern hill for much of the time but perhaps now and then, on a calm day, he did descend the cliff and cross the waist and the rock bridge, to build the southern cairn.

The summer after our trip with John Angus, Brian and I were alone again in the *Heather*. We had already been across the Minch to Skye and back, and out to St Kilda and back. The weather was beautifully fine and so, faithful to our axiom, we came out of the Sound, intending a trip down the west side to Causamul and the Monach Isles. But the tinker was beckoning. I had that little drystone bothy so clearly in mind, and I wanted to dig it out.

The sea really was calm when we arrived at Haskeir for the third time; we stopped, rolling lightly on the deep dark water. This time we sought to bypass the awkward overhang and looked for a landing place on the north hill itself. We pushed very close in, until the boat had only just room to swing, but still had to anchor in thirteen fathoms. We rowed like a couple of trippers up to the natural arch and back and chose a place below the fulmars' cliff where a sloping rock covered with seaweed and mussels made a nice natural jetty – at that moment of falling tide – and allowed the dinghy to be hauled up. It was easy, and a delight to make free with a place so often unapproachable, where a boat had no business to be; but the undercurrent of anxiety remained, as usual. First one left the big boat, whose anchor had only to trip off into deeper water, then one hauled up the dinghy high and dry and left it, hoping for the best when the time came to launch again. When we next saw Murdo Macdonald of Leverburgh, who spent his working life among horrible rocks, he agreed. It was all right as long as you stayed on board.

We worked upwards through the fulmar colony and found that our day (July 2nd) was their moment of hatching. There were eggs still smooth and glossy, eggs chipping, eggs half hatched, chicks still wet and chicks dry and fluffy up to two or three days old.

We walked about on the plateau amongst the sea-pink and the beds of plantain, visited the auks' ledges and the puffinry, and went to see the guillemots one could walk to, in a crack at the north end.

Now for the bothy. There it was, the oblong of stones below the rocky knoll, the floor thickly green with orache and sea campion, a doorway at the north end, a fulmar's nest and egg against one wall. The doorway was three feet wide with two lintel slabs still in position over it; the interior was just over seven feet long by five feet across. I put the fulmar's egg on one side and set to digging the peaty floor. The walls were amateurishly built, leaning inwards a little and mostly only one stone thick; but building it must have been a big job for one man. The stones I dug out included many flat slabs but not enough to account for a roof; that could have been a tarpaulin stretched over a few timber rafters. I threw out a cartload of peaty stuff, and got down to the footing of the walls and to a roughly paved stone floor. There were traces of charcoal among the stones and that was all; underneath them was clean grey sand.

Digging was a long hot job in the confined space. While I was at it Brian had another try for petrels, pulling up thrift clumps and overturning moveable stones and boulders, but without result. Now and then one or other of us walked across to make sure of boat and dinghy. It was warm and still on top of Haskeir; the sea became marked with the streaky patterns of calm under an overcast sky. A rock pipit's nest and eggs near the bothy seemed inland and quietly domestic after the rough exposure of sea birds. Above and behind the bothy were a couple of small and very unpleasant pools. The peat was a foot or two deep on the plateau – it must be a morass in winter – and the beds of sea plantain were as pure and lush as on the seal wallows at the other end of the island. I wondered whether after all seals might not get up there – somehow.

I dug away all the afternoon. By time I had finished the best height of wall from parapet to uncovered floor was four feet. I climbed out and looked down into it from the knoll; I

61

was loth to leave it, but it had given up no secrets, and staring wouldn't make it. So we left it, the parapet built up with peat-stained excavated stones, a cartload of peat alongside, and the fulmar's egg restored to a new nest.

Brian landed me on the south block and went off fishing. Once again I passed the tumult of terns – it was now mostly downy chicks on the ground – and crossed the rock bridge. The virulent pool had two eiders swimming on it. There was nothing new except a raven, a dead barnacle goose and a party of turnstones, but it was a pleasure to be back. I followed the rocky drain down from the wallows and visited the big fulmar colony on the corner cliff. I went to the cairn and looked northward along the length of the island; what a strange place. While I was there I mended the cairn.

From Haskeir we removed to romantic-sounding Causamul, an islet eight miles to southward and within two miles of the Uist coast.

From westward it looked as if the swell was going to cause difficulty, but once we had got round the back, on the landward side, it was very different. Causamul itself is only a low mound about a hundred yards across and thirty feet high; the character of the place comes from the reef, a fine expanse of rock stretching away to the north, taking the ocean swell on one side but full of quiet leads and lagoons on the other. Landing, for boats or for seals, was much easier than the look of the chart suggested. Causamul in fact – the islet itself, the reef with its channels and creeks and with extensive platforms remaining above high water – seemed an idealized site for a seal colony, except for being too near the mainland. At least fifty seals were taking a keen interest in our visit, an unusually high count for any seal resort in the summertime. The slopes of the main islet were patched with small dry-bottomed wallows; the rest was a thicket of mayweed full of nesting eider ducks. There was even an area of rough matted grass, also occupied by eiders, and a really well made summit cairn. A few puffins and black guillemots – missing from Haskeir –

were nesting among boulders, and one or two fulmars were prospecting.

We went on southwards to find a night's anchorage at the Monach Isles. On the way we passed inside Deasker, the last of the fringe of rocky islets lying off the Atlantic coast of North Uist. This one is a low skerry and was so thickly covered with cormorants, tall and black, in silhouette, that it looked as if they were standing on a raft.

At midnight we anchored in Croic Harbour, a euphemism for a wide, shallow and now glassy sheet of water, half-enclosed by a crescent of sand and dunes, palely visible in the twilight.

The Monach Isles show what the Hebridean climate can do with bare shell sand. Though they have a backbone of rock the three islands are essentially one great sand dune three miles long. The high surrounding dunes are capped with marram grass and scooped into bare sand cliffs by the wind; the interior is a wide plain of sweet smelling flowery machair. The main island Ceann Ear is joined by sandy fords, first to Shivinish and then on westwards to Ceann Iar; they are, as Martin said, 'of the same mould with the big island'. At either end are two rocky outriders, Stockay to the east and Shillay with the lighthouse to the west.

The islands used to support a community of crofters, rearing cattle and growing barley. There was almost a village on Ceann Ear. I had been to the islands once before and had camped for a few days on the big island. At this time, shortly before the war, two shepherding families were still in residence. Flocks of sheep roamed the machair and the shepherds went on horseback. There was a school and a little church; the lighthouse was manned and lit; small boats came up through the fords from Grimsay for summer lobstering. Apart from the lighthouse only the big island was occupied and the only other house was an empty cottage on Ceann Iar, nearly a two mile walk from the settlement by way of the tidal fords. I remembered that romantic cottage standing alone in the dunes and looking across the blue bay; I remembered spinning a fancy about living there for a summer.

In daylight we found ourselves anchored in front of the cottage – a ruin. We rowed ashore to go there first and as we stepped in there was a rush of wings and a buzzard flew out. The nest was a pile of dried laminaria stalks, inaccessible up among rotting rafters. A fulmar was nesting in the hearth and another sat upstairs on the flapping remains of the bedroom floor.

The islands had long lain desolate, the lighthouse unlit, but small boats with two-man-crews still came from Grimsay for the summer lobstering and shacked up in derelict houses and bothies. The real inhabitants were now fulmars, as we realized as soon as we walked round the dunes of Ceann Iar. But fulmars belong to sea cliffs and remote rocks; they made a strange impression here, beating and planing over the dunes in enigmatic silence. There must have been nearly a hundred nests on the island. Except for a few sites in fallen walls, all the eggs were laid on bare sand, some as far as two hundred yards inland and some up to four feet inside wind scooped tunnels in the face of the dunes. None of the eggs was hatched or even chipping, and there were plenty of sites with a bird sitting, but no egg. This dramatic colonization must have been both very recent and quick; only six years earlier a naturalists' check had not revealed a single bird. The island hardly seemed wild enough for this remarkable invasion, appearing both vulnerable and incongruous. The islands were by no means forgotten; sheep still grazed the machair and there were lobstermen about (though the young men we met later on appeared to be as dumb as the fulmars). Even hoodie crows were now nesting in the dunes, their nests, like the buzzard's, made of dried laminaria stalks.

We needed water and went looking for various old wells marked on the chart. The first was an overgrown puddle with an eel in it, others had drifted full of sand, but then we found a most splendid construction, perhaps once a reserve supply for the lighthouse on Shillay, though on the wrong side of the wide open sound between the two islands. A steep flight of mossy steps led deep down into the ground and at the bottom was a circular stone well with three feet of clear water in it.

There had once been a settlement on this corner of the island. The graveyard was a row of mounds in the dunes, each with a rough slab at either end. A boat cove faced the Sound of Shillay. Some ruined bothies remained and various banks and enclosures; in spite of the sand the onetime fields were spongy and peat was forming.

On the big island, Ceann Ear, one of the Grimsay lobstermen was demolishing the wee church – as he said – using the timber to make lobster store pots. The tattered blackboards on the walls of the school house were scribbled only with lobstermen's names, but the school books still lay about, just as in the St Kilda schoolroom after the evacuation. And as on St Kilda, it was the works of McDougall that teased the young. We browsed through the children's script books with the lofty sentiments partly copied out. 'Never listen to slander', they were admonished; I was surprised what tiny mistakes were marked.

We took the *Heather* round to Shillay and came into Pol Ban, the little boat harbour, by the leading marks on Eilean Siorruidh, Eternal Island – two stone beacons with their topmarks gone. Lighthouse and living quarters were certainly meant to be closed. Each door and window was blocked up with heavy galvanized sheets cemented in place, the chimneys were wired over, the yard fenced against sheep. The great tower of weathered red brick soared magnificently 150 feet above. Shillay was rock and dark green grass, heavily stocked with sheep. A couple of uninviting bothies were occupied by lobstermen. It could have been a seal island; it was connected to an area of reef and lagoons, there was a pond, and easy landings.

In the evening on our way northwards we passed Deasker again. It was too good a chance to miss in a glassy sea and there would never be another, so we headed in, dropped anchor, and rowed ashore without a care; we even left the dinghy afloat. Coming up from the south what had looked like a sand beach had been showing against the rock. It turned out to be a steep bank of shingle – big white pebbles – a feature unique amongst these rock-bound Atlantic islets.

The surface of Deasker was entirely given over to cormorants, the rock was plastered white throughout a slum of some seventy nests, the birds pressed together in a mob. The young stood as tall and dark as their parents and were ready to go. As we arrived they earnestly started being sick and many went flapping and splashing away through the muck.

Deasker is only about ten feet high. The sea washes over it in winter, and the *Pilot* says, adding, in a rare nature note 'but in June the sea swallows find it sufficiently dry to deposit their eggs'. A single pair of arctic terns squawked overhead and we found one oyster catcher's egg on the shingle. Two seals attended us and that was about all, except that a few tufts of vegetation, flecked with cormorants' down, had managed to find a hold in some of the highest clefts.

All through the evening as we plodded northwards the visibility was ominously clear. The islands and stacs of St Kilda stood needle sharp in the west, the black pencil of the Monach lighthouse was far astern and at different points of the compass lay the rocks of Deasker, Causamul and Haskeir: we had been to all five of them within a week.

St Kilda is a law unto itself and the Monach Isles are overcome by sand but the other three revealed a surprising diversity even in structure. Deasker has its shingle bank, Causamul its low reef, Haskeir its arches and caverns. Even the vegetation showed no pattern; chance was the sower and sooner or later some seed fell into good ground – such as it was – but plenty of arrivals must have had the chance and failed to keep a footing. Causamul had sixteen different species within its small compass, Haskeir had twelve and Deasker five. Only two plants were common to all three rocks (orache and mayweed); and only seven were common to both Haskeir and Causamul. Only Deasker and Causamul had docks (*Rumex crispus*); the Causamul wallows had toad rush and chickweed, the Haskeir wallows neither. Haskeir had sea plantain en masse but no buckshorn plantain; Causamul had buckshorn but no sea plantain. Haskeir had two grasses and no pasture, Causamul had three and a grassy mattress; and so on. Deasker's solitary speciality was the commonest of weed grasses, *Poa annua*; Haskeir's five specialities included the *Juncus tenuis* and *Triglochin maritima* by the little pool and Causamul's seven included silverweed, black oats and common spike-rush.

As for birds, Haskeir of course was special for fulmars, Deasker for cormorants, Causamul for eiders; but as with the plants nothing stood still. The short history of naturalists' visits to Haskeir is long enough to reveal plenty of comings and goings. In Harvie-Brown's day (1881) Haskeir was crowded with puffins, 'hundreds of eggs might have been gathered'; in 1939 they were 'entirely absent' and in our day we reckoned on about fifty pairs. Eiders were 'very plentiful' for Harvie-Brown but there were none at all in 1939. Arctic terns had a large colony in 1868 and again in our years of 1952-3, but they were missing in 1881 and in 1939. Fulmars (as elsewhere) have been the only consistent expansionists. The rocks may be changeless but not the life they support.

We entered the Sound of Harris again in darkness, with the sand beaches of Pabbay and Berneray showing pale on either hand. Doubtfully and then distinctly we picked up the northern sands and rocks of Ensay and headed hopefully towards the unrelieved blackness of Harris. Luckily we got a sight of Volinish beacon and hastily put ourselves on the right side of it. After that it was home-coming to Leverburgh at one o'clock in the morning; and then came the gale warnings.

# FIVE

◆

# *Summer in the Sound*

Roneval, the highest hill of south Harris, is only 1,500 feet high and flat topped but the summit is such a barren waste of loose bare stones that even in summer it looks as if snow patches should be lying there.

This modest hilltop must be as fine a vantage point as anywhere in the Outer Isles and all the way round the view carries to a far horizon. North-westwards lies the extra-ordinary rocky wilderness of the Forest of Harris and beyond rise the Clisham and the big hills of North Harris: north-eastwards the view goes far up the Minch to the Shiant Isles, twenty-five miles away, and to a sea horizon beyond: Skye and the Cuillins fill the south-east. The west is all Atlantic, marked on a good day with the ultimate dots of the Flannans, St Kilda, Haskeir. South-westwards, beyond the Sound, is North Uist, as much water as land and looking from this aerial perch like a vast floating bog. Near to, beyond the lesser bumps of Strondeval and Ben Obbe, the beloved Sound lies wide open.

At high tide the Sound is a sheet of water dotted with islands. At low tide it is as the Reverend John Macleod, minister of Harris, saw it in the eighteenth century and wrote his description for vol. 10 of the *Statistical Account* (1794).

'From an eminence near the Sound may be had a very curious view of the odd intermixture of land, rock, and water, which fills the space betwixt the mainland of Uist and the mainland of Harris. Standing on this eminence, at lowest

68

ebb in spring tides, and in calm weather, one contemplates with amazement the vast variety of islands, rocks, banks, shoals, and streights, before him, compares them to the stars in the galaxy, and is almost bewildered in the view . . . Here the tide rises to a great height; the current runs with amazing rapidity; the surge, when the wind blows against the tide, swells prodigiously; and the roar of the breakers, foaming over the banks and shoals to an immense distance, seems to threaten the islanders with a general deluge.'

Captain H. C. Otter RN directed the first survey of the Sound in 1857. The elegant chart, embellished with Views from Seaward and with engravings of St Clement church, Rodel, and of the two great iron beacons, was published two years later. Captain Otter's ship, HMS *Porcupine*, steam and sail, lay for a year in Bays Loch, Berneray, during the survey. He was still spoken of in Berneray, though the stories were dying out. Once the ship had to clear out of Village Bay, St Kilda, in a bad gale; she was laid on her beam ends and showed no signs of recovering. Two Boreray men were his pilots then, they cut away the lee side boats and managed to get her back with a bit of canvas. They were considered to have saved the ship.

The great days of Boreray are long gone, the seafaring tradition, the prosperity of Martin's time, and long before that the fame of the island's Monks' Field 'for all the Monks that dyed in the Islands that lye Northward from Egg were buried in this little plot . . .' Nowadays Berneray people pointed to the small low island two miles westward and spoke with a smile of the 'King of Boreray', for a single family farmed the island and inhabited the last house.

Boreray seemed an ulikely base for seafaring men, with a rock-bound coast facing the Atlantic and shoal water and sandy strands on the landward side. There was no sheltered anchorage and no sort of harbour, not even a boat cove. A vessel could anchor close off Lingay, to the southward, but, said the *Pilot*, 'it is advisable to stop off the entrance to the channel and wait for a pilot, who will come off from Boreray on the pilot signal being made, if the sea is not too high'.

69

When Brian and I anchored off Boreray and rowed ashore it was a Sunday, but the windows of the church were blind or boarded up, the interior was full of fallen plaster and laths, the enclosure was in use as a sheep fank. Groups of ruined black houses nearby told of the population of former days. We found Martin's cup-marked stones: 'the Tradition is that these Vacuities were dug for receiving the Monks knees when they prayed upon 'em'. Boggy bordered Loch Mor was lively with phalaropes. The loch has a mysterious underground passage leading to the sea; 'one of the Inhabitants called *Mack-vanish*, i.e. *Monks-Son*', said Martin, 'had the curiosity to creep naked through this Passage'. Dogs ran out barking from the last house, a tin roofed bungalow. 'They' were all indoors, peering out of the windows and no doubt consumed with curiosity. We felt guilty, walking past, desecrating the Sabbath when one either stayed indoors or went to church; we left without making contact.

Boreray men among others no doubt accompanied Captain Otter's surveyors and helped with place names. All the main island names are Norse, which shows who effectually got there first. By no means all the rest are Gaelic though many must be literal translations to the English chart; a key danger like Rough Black Rock is an obvious example. Captain Otter surprisingly did not leave his own name in the Sound – it is well remembered in his other surveys in the West of Scotland – but his surveyors left theirs: Lieutenant A. Dent of Dent Shoal, Messrs Stanton and Stanley RN of Stanton Channel and Stanley Rock, Mr Cramer of Cramer Rock. It looks as if they added more names as they went along, One Eye Island perhaps, or Guy Rocks, Mast Rock and Black Mast Rock, or simply Half Channel Rock, but in most cases it is impossible to tell which English names are theirs and which are translations. Did they go aground on Boat Rock? Seal, Great Seal and Little Seal could reflect the shape of the rocks, or record traditional hauling out places for grey seals. Many islets were left un-named, inviting any navigator to choose his own (which we ourselves did, inventing such nonsense as Frying Pan Island, because someone happened to be holding one as we went by, or Emperor Isle because of two emperor moth caterpillars found in the heather when we landed to explore). But what should be made of Oil, Splears, Crago, Oidre, the Cabbage Group . . .?

The big island of Berneray, in effect an extension of North Uist, still had a straggling village, church, school, two shops and some three hundred inhabitants. For the rest there were the shepherds of Pabbay and sometimes a couple of cattlemen on Killegray and Ensay, and that was all. The Mansion House of Killegray and the grander one of Ensay both stood echoing empty.

As for the tides, filling and emptying the Sound, Captain Otter left his testament, couched in the stately style of the day: 'It may be generally stated that in summer, in neap tides, the stream comes from the Atlantic during the whole of the day, and from the Minch during the whole of the night. In winter this precept is nearly reversed. In spring tides both of summer and winter the stream sets in from the Atlantic during the greater part of the time the water is rising, but never for more then 5¼ hours, and it flows back into the Atlantic during most of the fall of the tide. Where the water is confined by rocks and islands, such as inside of Stromay Red Rock etc., the velocity is nearly 5 knots an hour during springs, and not much less during neaps, whilst in other places it does not exceed a rate of 2 to 2½ knots.'

A century after Captain Otter the Sound was surveyed all over again, by HM Ships *Cook* and *Shackleton*. The new chart is on a smaller scale and so congested with soundings that in spite of modern colour washes it is much less easy to read than the old and lacks the grace and delicacy of fine nineteenth-century engraving. Captain Otter's chart remains the best counsellor and guide for any sort of boat as well as being a collector's piece and a work of art. But the new surveyors did find some new underwater rocks.

The maze and medley of the Sound does admit of some classification. Captain Otter broke it into groups, the Saghay group, the Carminish Islands, Groay group, Hermetray group, the Cabbage group. The old *Pilot* – carried on from Captain

Otter's original sailing directions – even recommended anchorage alongside the Cabbage group, a litter of rocks above and below water in the middle of the Sound, though why any vessel should want to go near such a place is hard to tell.

With a length of thirty-six feet and beam of twelve, the *Heather* was much too big and clumsy for the minor boat channels, and our little dinghy too small for anything but landings and short range explorations. The *Pilot*'s recurring refrains 'available for', 'useful for', 'only suitable for boats with local knowledge', roundly contradicted itself in the case of one hair-raising channel, 'through which a vessel must be conned by eye from the masthead'. This sort of talk, which made the old *Pilot* so entertaining, and useful, has not surprisingly been dropped from modern editions.

All the same, at one time or another, as weather and a rising tide allowed, we did take the *Heather* through all the boat channels, through the six mile dog-legged length of Grey Horse Channel, through Gunwale Channel (well named!), through Seolait Mhic Neacail and all the rest. 'When is the best time to get through the Reef?' we asked in Berneray. 'Never!' Most extraordinary of all channels was the straight rock-sided corridor of Rangas, one mile long, which disappears without trace at high tide. The one time purpose of this gut must have been to provide part of a sheltered inshore route for boats working along the coastline of North Uist. The *Pilot* gave it a least depth of three feet but when we came to give it a try at low water of a spring tide, laminaria was showing all across. We stopped and let the boat drift in on the flood. There was a gentle bump and bump again and then she stuck. It was an hour before the tide lifted her off and then as she swung clear the boulders that had held her glistened below among the weed, and the propeller fouled instantly. Once inside there was no way out but on, along a narrow water road as straight as a ruler and with no room to turn. There was nothing for it but to clear the propeller and creep warily along the temporary canal between the seaweed covered rock walls rising high on either side. Once was enough. All these channels have disappeared from the modern chart; congestion left no room for them anyway.

The one and only sign of the times was the establishment of a brand new track straight through the middle of the Sound – Cope Passage. It was marked by a perfect avenue of fifteen buoys, nearly all of them lit, and its purpose was to make an easy route through the Sound for the Army landing craft on its way to serve the garrison of St Kilda. The traditional tracks along the Harris shore were too difficult and dog-legged.

During the old *Heather*'s very last cruise in 1959, and on a grey and drizzly day, Brian and I became dutiful tourists and followed through the new track, ticking off the buoys one by one. It was like driving along a road. We left Gousman on one hand and the littered rocks of the Cabbage group on the other; the buoys led on to pass the eastern end of Berneray, with Pabbay beyond. The last pair of buoys made a gateway; they floated quietly in innocent-looking water but each bore the sinister word 'BAR': 'the bar between Berneray and Killegray is generally marked by overfalls, breaks in heavy weather and is reported to dry occasionally'. After all those nice new buoys the new channel was just for slack high water. We went through without touching.

We made our anchorages in Cheese Bay and Calm Bay of North Uist, in the Basin of Vaccasay, in the Basin (of Opsay and Sarstay), in a bight in the coast of Hermetray, in Bays Loch, Berneray, and in Loch na Ban.

The shallow quarter-mile width of Loch na Ban, indenting the northern corner of the North Uist shore, was all right the first time but the next year when we tried it again, it was not. After a night of wind and rain we woke to some ominous bumps and looked out to find our precious vessel settling comfortably among seaweed-covered boulders, while dinghy and painter lay neatly astern as if on tow. The tide continued to retreat for another two hours so there was plenty of time to make arrangements, to recover the fouled anchor at low water and to lay it again by dinghy with all the cable and rope we could muster, to lay a small kedge as well, and to haul all taut. The stranded boat looked horribly conspicuous but somehow or other we managed to get her off, without damage and without being spotted. It was another Sunday.

Grey Horse Channel leads in from the Minch, between Hermetray and Greanem, between State Rock and Staffin Skerry, between Opsay and Oil and into the Basin. The way on and out led narrowly between two islets and on the top of the port hand islet stood Grey Horse in person, a tumbling cairn of grey stones bearded with lichen, surrounded by ragged robin flowering in ungrazed grass; beyond lay the dog-legged course of four miles across open water to Bays Loch, Berneray.

In all the Sound, the Basin was the place. As an anchorage it remained tentative; it was encumbered with rocks and the bottom was very uneven, either too deep or too shallow, either mud or rock. It was cosy enough at low water within the encircling reefs but most of the shelter disappeared at high tide when nothing was left but a ring of detached islets. In threatening weather we went elsewhere but over the years I came to associate the Basin with quiet days and ambitious dinghy excursions. I knew it on and off for ten years.

The tide ebbed and all around the Basin a new world of wet rock and weed rose into the air, hills and dales swathed in glistening seaweed. The different floor levels made innumerable lagoons and pools that began to empty as soon as they formed, running out in little rivers and waterfalls. The pools were full of sea anemones. Bone white rock that looked so sharkishly sinister under water came up encrusted with barnacles. The earliest uncovered weed began to darken and dry, some of the shell-floored channels were reduced to wading depth, laminaria and thong weed flopped awash in the last of the ebb. When I stood by Grey Horse and looked back, the anchored *Heather* seemed to have found a last boat pool; from the dinghy she was lost, her masts stuck out from a wilderness of rock and weed.

The tide turned, the water seeped back with a dusty scum on it; the dried bladders of weed floated lightly, swelled and

paled and went awash, and submerged in their proper element. The deception of harmless open water was restored.

The Basin and its surrounding area of islands and islets,
reefs and skerries and fields of seaweed revealed itself as an
undiscovered sanctuary. I had guessed at it from the look of
the chart, and so it turned out to be. Long sought Narstay
waited within easy dinghy range but something longer sought
came first. Two animal heads moved across the Basin, a
smaller following a larger: common seal and pup.

This really was 'at last'. Grey seals one kept on meeting but
common seals had always remained elusive. From one end of
the Hebrides to the other we had only ever come across them
as a couple of corpses on the beach, one on Berneray, the
other sixty miles away on Vatersay, Barra. Otherwise there
was only a solitary and very young pup, floundering on the
surface and unable to dive, which we nearly ran down as once
we tickled into the rock-strewn and highly un-navigable
lagoon in Hellisay, Sound of Barra. That was all. Now here
they were at last, chubby, biscuit-coloured, pug-faced little
seals plentiful and at home in their own place. And when we
did row over to Narstay and land, the island and its nearby
skerries and waterways turned out to be evidently their headquarters in the Sound.

There was nothing wrong with Narstay, indeed it was
rather nice, except for all its defensive rocks. It was an
ordinary sort of dull-looking grassy island with a few sheep
on it; kidney-shaped, about three hundred yards long, no
more than thirty feet high, and bounded by a rocky seaweed-
covered shoreline. But it was one of those places where
something was always happening. The short spongy turf was
littered with new and old droppings and flight feathers of
greylag geese. It was roosting as well as grazing ground, judging by the groups of heaped-up droppings. When the artist
John Robinson was crewing with us one year, and we stepped
into Narstay, he at once picked up a goose quill and sharpened
it and sat down to his pen and ink sketching. We seldom
glimpsed the geese themselves. A strange-looking duck fluttered from a stinking pool with half a dozen ducklings

75

tumbling after her – shoveler and her brood. Herons waded among low water boulders; one could look back to Tahay a mile away and make out the dark dots of rowan bushes in the little cliff where a few nests were perched; it was the only heronry we knew of in the Sound. On a grey day nothing could have been more brilliant than a bunch of oyster catchers standing on newly uncovered weed. Shelduck and ducklings cruised by, eider ducks and their amalgamated broods floated in seaweed awash, a pair of mergansers passed in line ahead, gannets were fishing the deeps further out. Terns settled and uprose again from a rocky knoll where the yellow lichen was bright as paint. Turnstones were flipping over the wet weed, a summer flock of starlings probed the grass of Narstay Beag, shags made a frieze on a nearby skerry. The ceaseless patrol of carking gulls went on overhead, and below lay flattened nests and crab litter. Grey seals lay out on Parliament Rock to the north-west, a bare backed skerry splashed white by shags; seals' song carried down on the breeze as if it were autumn. Common seal bulls and cows and pups cruised at the surface or lay hauled out on weed and rock. Safe in the water they had all the curiosity of grey seals; a cow's head in full face view, watching in interested enquiry, looked just like a six week old grey seal pup in his play pool; both appeared to have full binocular vision. But they were much more shy than greys and when they were hauled out, to show oneself at a hundred yards range was enough to start them slithering.

H. Hesketh Prichard, author of *Sport in wildest Britain*,* said that he had never seen common seals in the Hebrides hauled out except on rock; elsewhere they belong to sand-banks. In either case they like to allow themselves to be stranded by the ebb tide; they are not nearly such climbers as grey seals and have much less to do with dry land. In Harvie-Brown's time common seals were very abundant, 'perhaps nowhere more so than in the Sound of Harris' but . . . 'the Sound of Harris had become, to a large extent, depopulated

* *Sport in Wildest Britain* by H. Hesketh Pritchard (Heinemann, London, 1921)

by 1886. This is owing principally to the short-sighted policy of a "general merchant" in that district, and to the issue of some thirty gun licences now taken out in North Uist alone. The island of Berneray, too, at the present time swarms with guns, and under these circumstances it is not rash to predict the speedy and utter extermination of the seals'. In our day a wary population of perhaps fifty animals was centred round Narstay. In the Hebrides at least, common seals and common gulls share the same misnomer.

Narstay had fifteen sheep on it and offlying Narstay Beag (our name) had three. (It really isn't difficult for an Englishman to name unnamed islands in the language of the country, though the spelling may go awry.) Adder's tongue fern grew in the wet turf; rough grass was pink with ragged robin, pink stonecrop coloured the rocks. Long abandoned peat workings had grown over with swathes of waving bog cotton: grassy banks of indecipherable earthworks were well enough drained to be white with clover. A row of green tumuli, where an occasional stone showed through, must once have been lively summer shielings; beds of nettles about them testified to long gone habitation.

I sat myself down one day on the rocks facing Narstay Beag as the ebb began and watched the grand emptying process get under way. Below me was a narrow, sand-floored submarine valley, walled with rock and weed, the water clear as crystal. An enormous grey seal bull came drifting down the gut as near and as plain to see as if he were in an aquarium, his front flippers steering, his hindquarters waving fishlike from side to side, generating an effortless thrust – a diagramatic exposure of underwater swimming. His great roman nose broke surface for a breath, he looked twice the size of the common seals.

Grey seals travel according to season, but all these submarine valleys among the rocks was home ground for the resident common seals. They must have known them generation after generation, as the local boatmen knew their own ways on the surface above, and as we know the roads to the station.

Common and grey seals have such different arrangements: common seal pups shed their white coats in utero, they are born in summer ready to swim away and they are suckled for a month or more.

The immediate contrast between the two species, in their respective breeding seasons, was that mother and pup of common seals had the felicity of play; and happy it looked. It was charming to watch pup swimming close behind mother, trying to climb on her back or making puppyish mock bites, with mouth closed, at her head. Sometimes when a pup was nearly submerged and nudging at mother's flank, it looked as if it was trying to suckle under water. Mothers really did have something more to do with their pups than merely suckle them, and this no doubt was because of protracted suckling and the pups' precocious swimming. And the pups played with water on their own, splashing and flapping, rolling on their backs, trying to dive. They 'bottled' – hung vertically in the water, nose to sky – and let themselves sink.

Ashore, as mother lay on her side and pup searched for the teats, I was amused to see an exact repeat of grey seal behaviour, the identical, irritable-looking whirring of the cow's free flipper, as if signing to the pup 'further back, further back'. The fattest cows were multi-chinned; the smaller the pup, the fatter the mother, just like greys; one blew up as the other subsided. The cows' parental attentions can have left them little opportunity for feeding during lactation. Like grey seals the adults lay restless and itchy, with an occasional armless humping shift of position, or fast asleep; but the perpetual bickering of greys was missing. They were nearly silent; all I heard from the adults was generalized animal grunts. The pups' babyish, throaty, pathetic wailing had something of calf, something of humanity in it, much like the crying of grey seal pups but less realistically human.

The same difficulty over coat colour arose as with greys. Sleek and wet they were all much alike, dry and fluffy they had the same sort of colour range as greys; mottled and brindled, from iron-grey to moth-eaten brown, paler towards biscuit, ruddier towards chestnut. Monkey-faced little seals in shades of biscuit was a fair generalisation.

Just as many islands as those we set foot on remained untrodden and unknown. All that we did know had some speciality or other but the wildlife they supported was often secret. Scatological evidence always lay in abundance, the traces of geese, otters, rats and of miscellaneous unknowns, but the makers thereof often remained unseen. Always there was evidence of rats. Greater black-backed gulls were overnumerous but it was alien rats that spoilt the innocence of the islands; there can be no Garden of Eden where rats infest. At least the glimpses we had of them were of rufous brown, instead of dirty grey. They must have originally spread and colonized the Sound from human habitation on either side. They were shore-based and evidently moved freely from island to island. An area of foreshore turf was hummocked and riddled with burrows, yet as often as not tern colonies with eggs and running chicks survived alongside. We picked up sticks of driftwood and dug in the peaty turf, but never found more than dirty pads of grass and crab remains; I bought and set a break-back trap but it vanished overnight. When we explored the tiny natural fort of Dun, 200 yards off the Uist shore, the grassy summit had just suffered an invasion of rats. A little forest of flowering angelica had stood there but now every stalk lay felled and wilting and the crown of each root had been gnawed out. Four years later all that survived of the angelica was a few small leaves in the grass. When I walked the cliff edge of next-door Groatay a fine buzzard flew out, then I found scattered duck down and bird remains, then bits of rabbits, then half a fresh rat, then the trodden empty nest in the low cliff, then another half rat. Another time when I walked round the cliffs of Hermetray, next in line, and found the buzzard's nest I was gratified to see the two young birds surrounded with bits of rats and nothing else. At the other end of the Sound another pair of buzzards frequented the low island of Torogay, off ill-starred Loch na Ban. It appeared to be only a sitting out place but the sheep grazed turf was dotted with part rats. Evidently the resident buzzards of the Sound made their living from rats as much as from anything else.

Each end of the Minch entry to the Sound is marked by a Dun. The little Dun off the Uist shore showed tumbled remains of artifact stones on the summit and the remains of a ring of drystone walling round the base, but the other Dun, the bare rock stac of Dun-aarin, eighty seven feet high, ('conspic.'), was entirely natural – a seamark leading into the main channel off the Harris shore. It was long enough before we found a day to anchor off familiar Dun-aarin and land at last but then only to find it dull: white splashed ledges from which the auks had already gone, and not much else. It looked such a fine craggy place.

Between these two boundary stones, and reading from Dun to Dun-aarin, comes, first, Groatay, then the Hermetray group, then isolated Gousman further in, then the Groay group (Groay, Gilsay, Lingay, Scaravay), then Dun-aarin with Big and Little Gomersom and Cletha Medha and Langay backing up behind. The Groay group looked like a dull lot of sheep islands and remained unexplored. Gousman, bang in the middle of the Minch end of the Sound, lay alongside the avenue of new buoys. Gousman was particular for its densely grown crown of flowering scabious and for otter habitation. There was an otter holt above a brackish pool, the bare black peat was worn with otter slides and tunnels and dotted with middens of fish scales and fishy spraint, the grass was flattened with runways and landings. A guyed pole on the summit with a white wooden diamond topmark lined up with the summit cairn of Killegray three miles beyond, and led in to the buoyed channel. Gousman supported four sheep.

The big island of Hermetray, three-quarters of a mile long, was famous to us for the right-angled bight in its sheltered side, the cosiest anchorage in all the Sound, but once inside and round the corner there was barely room to swing. Hermetray had a proper inland loch, long abandoned peat banks and ruined stone bothies of beehive type. 'I saw here', said Martin, 'the foundation of a House built by the *English*, in

K. *Charles* the First's time, for one of their Magazines to lay
up the Cask, Salt, &. for carrying on the Fishery, which was
then begun in the Western Islands, but this design miscarried
because of the Civil Wars, which then broke out.' Sheep and
a couple of sheep fanks, one with a new concrete dip built on,
were the only marks of today.

The small island of Groatay, alongside Hermetray and as
high, was notable for a detached rock stac, very good for
amateur climbing, and considered by Captain Otter to be
worth marking on his chart.

The best islands were those within dinghy range of the
Basin – the encircling islands of Opsay, Sarstay, Oil, Grey
Horse and a dozen more unnamed, and the outliers Narstay,
Sursay, Vottersay, Tahay, Vaccasay. Tahay, the tallest of
them, (209 feet), was the one with the rowan trees and
herons' nests in a little cliff. Tahay had a sometime boat harbour enclosed with drystone walls and what had once been a
township of black houses; one ruin had been converted into
sheep works. The interior had inland cliffs and hilly tracts of
old heather, aromatic in the sun. If I were condemned to live
on an uninhabited island in the Sound I should choose
Tahay.

Sursay had the usual sheep fank and dip but also sedgy
tracts with whimbrel in residence. Vertical rock faces were
gardens of white stonecrop and tufts of bell heather and great
beards of grey lichen. Vottersay looked well on the chart but
was low-lying and dull, mostly close-cropped turf with the
regulation sheep fank and dip. When black-backed gulls ventured over Vaccasay they were met and mobbed and sent
packing by an angry crowd of terns and common gulls; as
long as they were numerous enough they could well defend
their property. Vaccasay was over-grazed and peaty, the
sheep fank was made of blocks of peat; the shore yielded
useful flotsam and jetsam. The islet Oil, shaped like a sport-
ive whale complete with tail flukes, appeared to be clothed in
a light brown haze, which turned out to be the tall dry stems
of flowering hair grass, a forest growing from its own self-

made soft mattress underfoot. Yet three sheep made a living there.

Like all the rest Sarstay had seen better days; seven forgotten bothies, shielings, byres – whatever they had been – seven grassy mounds stood in a row along the ridge, and modern Sarstay's few sheep were not keeping up with the good grazing. An adjacent islet had only a square yard or two of peaty turf above the boulders but it was entirely riddled by rats: Rat Isle, of course; somehow one doesn't care to go barefoot among rat burrows. Opsay, across the Basin, had the same grassy monuments as Sarstay, but shorn by geese, and was notable for a brackish lagoon and for otters. Signs of otters in the islands were as ubiquitous as those of rats but not until I stood on Opsay did I spy a small eared head, and then another, moving across the water, heading for Oil. I was mooring the dinghy to a stone on a minor detachment of Opsay when I saw the next one, coming straight towards me. He came on unseeing, eyes, ears, whiskers all plain, back awash, a little bow wave on either side; perhaps like a running hare unable to see straight ahead. He made to land at my feet, alongside the dinghy – sleek wet fur, half out of the water and weed: an instant stare, an instantaneous silent disappearance, and never a curious head to bob up further out and look back like a seal.

The ruined black houses, the grassy mounds, the bog cotton waving over ancient peat banks were repeated again and again. And Martin had said of Hermetray that it 'affords great plenty of Milk in *January* and *February* beyond what can be seen in the other Islands'. What a traffic of boats there must have been in days of yore, what a ferrying of cattle and calves, of cheese and butter: peat smoke rising from the islands, ragged children running barefoot in the grass. 'No more, oh nevermore!'

Nowadays was represented only by sheep and sheep works, but still on a very peasant scale; it was still considered worth while to stock a small islet with two or three sheep. The sheep had to be landed and taken off, gathered, shorn, dipped. There were boats in Berneray and at Leverburgh and Rodel on the Harris side. Every winter the local lobstermen worked inshore while their summer grounds were unapproachable, and they regularly cleared out the Sound by spring. But in all our summertimes there was never a man or a boat to be seen out amongst the islands. Well, hardly ever . . . Once there was a man in a rowing boat; he had lobster creels on board and mackerel in the boat, so we went where he'd been and got some too. We had the islands to ourselves.

During the *Heather*'s last cruise of all Brian and I came back across the Little Minch to the Sound, a long leg of nearly fifty miles from a visit to friends in the island of Soay, south of Skye. The low grey humps of the Outer Isles came up one after another until the whole seaward horizon was a grey barrier under a grey sky. We passed old Hermetray, cut in between State Rock and Staffin Skerry, between Oil and Opsay, and into the Basin – a homecoming! The sky suddenly lifted, a yellow evening sun broke through and stroked the sleeping mounds of Sarstay and Opsay; fleecy clouds stood as deep below the quiet water as high above. The ebb tide flowed silently by and out of the lagoon past crouched Grey Horse: seals' heads cruising, herons stalking the shallows, no sound but the raucous cries of gulls and terns. The Hebridean magic time came at midnight dusk, in breathless calm and glassy sea. *This* is the time an old man means when he starts his anecdote, 'It wass a pewtiful evening and I wass out in the poat . . .' and then in no time one is struggling off a lee shore with a stopped engine.

If we wanted to see a man on an island, or cattle instead of sheep, then it had to be on the rich sandy islands of Killegray and Ensay and Pabbay. Populous Berneray was a different case and really belonged to North Uist to which, in some indeterminate future, it might even be joined by a causeway. Berneray alone was lively, with church and school, post office and two shops, telephone kiosk and a mile of rough road. But within two years the number of working looms had dropped from thirteen to one and the dozen lobster boats of a few years past were reduced to three or four. The few children that were left went away for secondary education and did not return; there was simply no living to be had at home. But twenty-three houses had telephones; the alien network of poles and wire showed up from afar, above the indigenous thatch and stone of clustered black houses.

Berneray typified the 'dry' sort of Hebridean island, sandy or shallow of soil over the rock, short of peat and even of water. Cunningham's puffer brought coal to the jetty, horses and carts took it away. A splendid bunch of pale, long tailed horses ran loose up the hill.

Once a year summer communion was festival time in Berneray, Thursday to Sunday and two services a day. John Angus Patterson's *Dunbeath Castle* brought in boatloads of passengers for the occasion. Men, women and children in their best clothes thronged into the church. There was even a sprinkling of light coloured suits among the men's blue serge and bright coats among the women's prevailing black. Happening once to stem the procession straggling along the dusty road for the evening session we thus exchanged 'Fine day' with nearly every soul on the island.

The last time the *Heather* went to Berneray we found that the twenty year old joke about a promised new pier was at last over; Cunningham's puffer lay alongside it discharging coal, and we lay alongside her. But Roddy Maclean had retired and sold his boat. Only two lobster boats were working and not a single weaver; houses were falling empty; the island, like many another, lived on Public Assistance, new pier or not.

A couple of cattlemen stayed on Killegray now and then and the surgeon from Stornoway hospital brought his family and a cow and a rowing boat for the summer holidays and lived in the Mansion House. A row of unthinned lettuces in the sandy garden awaited their coming, but the weedy strawberries would be over. The eroding sand cliffs of Killegray uncovered little hearths of split and blackened stones; here was the far end of habitation in the island. A little scratching soon discovered bird, animal and fish bones, ash and bits of charcoal, shards of coarse fire-blackened pottery, a bit of flint, a bit of antler, seashells – limpet, winkle, razor shell, scallop, cockle. The ancient rubbish blackened one's hands.

The beautiful little bay on the east side of Ensay is enclosed by reefs on either hand with a crescent beach between them and the water lies green over white sand. It was probably from this very beach of 'the Isle *Esay* in *Harries*' that Martin embark'd for St Kilda, 'the *29th* of *May*, at Six in the Afternoon, 1697, the Wind at S.E. . . . .'

Concrete steps led up from the sand to a pair of stone gateposts and iron gates, to the front door of the grand Mansion House. The windows were blank with drawn blinds but the door was unlocked. Silence within the massive stone walls! In the hall a mouldy bull's head, some champion beast of old, gazed from the wall and continued to moulder. In the dank stone-flagged kitchen a row of bells dangled from rusty springs. Upstairs in the best bedroom stood a magnificent four-poster hung with tasselled velvet. Shelves of damp books in the library invited latterday browsing.

Three cattlemen – the reception committee – were staying in decrepit farm buildings alongside the mansion. There were bushes of veronica in the park at the back of the house and even a lingering apple tree against the wall. Elder, sycamore and fuchsia tried to be trees but salty winds had laid them near horizontal. The private chapel was almost dark inside with the furniture stacked on the sunken floor and only loopholes in the walls for light. Ensay has a notable standing stone on a knoll above the chapel; heathen stone and Christian cross were silhouetted together against the sky. Rain came down all day long.

The strands of Killegray and Ensay and all their incomparable colours of clean sea water over white shell sand carry through to Berneray with its two miles of dunes and great sand hill sixty feet high, and to Pabbay beyond. They come to an end in the little white beach and miniscule dunes of Shillay.

85

# SIX

◆

# *Seals' Fortunes*

'To the north-west of the Keantuach of Vyist lyis ane Ile be 12 mile of sea callit *Haifsker*, quhairin infinite slauchter of selchis is maid at certane times in the zeir . . .' Thus wrote Mr Donald Monro, High Dean of the Isles, who travelled through the Hebrides in 1549.

Gasker and Haskeir (but not Shillay) and Causamul – each in sight of the next – were for centuries the traditional sites of annual seal battues, when seal products were a much valued natural resource. Haskeir was foremost in the records.

John Monipenie, Scottish historian, wrote in 1612: 'Haniskera: about this island, at certaine times of the yeare, are many sealches; they are taken by the countrie men.'

George Buchanan, another historian, in 1751: 'Havelschyer, to which, at certain seasons of the year, many *Sea-calves* do resort, and are there taken.'

The seals of both Haskeir and Causamul were the perquisite of farms in North Uist. The Reverend Allan Macqueen, minister of North Uist, in his contribution to the old *Statistical Account* (1794) said that the two rocks were 'inhabited only by seals, which the possessors of the farms these rocks belong to, attempt to kill once a-year, either in the month of October or November; for this purpose, they use clubs or long sticks, heavy at the end, and with which they strike them on the head, a blow in any other part being ineffectual'. A subsequent minister, the Reverend Finlay M'Rae continued the tale in *The new Statistical Account of*

*Scotland* (1845) '. . . a boat is sent to each rock, the crew being furnished with large clubs which they use dexterously. When successful, the division is made according to ancient rule, with scarcely a murmur or dispute. The proprietor is entitled to four, and the minister to one seal. This the latter receives not as a title, but because the glebe comprehends a part of the farm which is entitled to a share of the rock'. At about the same time the naturalist John MacGillivray (1842) filled in the details: 'In the beginning of November a large boat filled with men leaves North Uist under night, and generally arrives at Haskir soon after daybreak. The men land upon the island armed with long clubs and separate into two bodies, one of which attacks the seals upon the shelving rocks upon which they are found lying with their cubs, while the other cuts off their retreat to the water. A short but fierce struggle then takes place; a few of the animals escape, the rest are killed by repeated blows about the root of the nose, their only vulnerable spot, and the rock is soon covered with the dying and the dead. About seventy are thus annually secured, but the number varies considerably, as many as 120 having sometimes been obtained . . .'

The same plan was followed at Causamul. In Martin's time 'the Rock Cousmil' belonged, like Haskeir, 'to the Farmers of the next adjacent Lands . . . These Farmers man their Boat with a competent number fit for the business, and they always imbark with a contrary wind, for their security against being driven away by the Ocean, and likewise to prevent them from being discovered by the Seals, who are apt to smell the scent of them, and presently run to sea'. As at Haskeir, the passes to the sea were manned 'and then the signal for the general attacque is given'. And as for the seals 'if they be not hit exactly on the front, they contract a Lump on their Forehead, which makes them look very fierce; and if they get hold of the Staff with their Teeth, they carry it along to Sea with them'. Martin was told that, '320 Seals Young and Old, have been killed at one time in this Place'.

Seals were also killed, but by a different method, at the Monach Isles. Judging by the name and by topography it was at the Monach Shillay that according to Martin, 'the Natives formerly killed many Seals in this manner, they twisted together several small Ropes of Horse Hair in form of a Net, contracted at one end like a Purse, and so by opening and shutting this Hair Net, these seals were catched in the narrow Channel'.

In 1858 the proprietor of North Uist, Sir John Orde, affronted by the annual slaughter, forbade any further expeditions to Haskeir; 'to which the men of Uist looked forward with great eagerness', according to the naturalist Captain H. J. Elwes. But the only result seems to have been that boats came from further afield, from Harris and even Lewis. Captain Elwes, who was on a tour of bird stations of the Outer Isles in 1868 and who got a boat to take him out to Haskeir on 30 June, estimated that the annual harvest of seals varied from forty to a hundred young and old.

J. A. Harvie-Brown naturally enough took in Haskeir in his day (1 June, 1881), during one of his many yacht cruises among the Outer Isles but in spite of deploring the decrease of the Haskeir seals which 'remains unimpeded, if not accelerated', one of his own objects was 'the "annexation" of a good specimen of the Grey Seal'. 'We saw some *great grey* monsters bobbing about in the white surf where no boat dared venture; one even came within 30 yards of the boat'; one of the sailors 'saluted him with a double discharge all at once, of an 8-bore gun! but did no damage except to himself'.

In the summer of 1898 V. H. Hesketh Pritchard landed twice on Haskeir to shoot seals for the Natural History Museum. He tried again in 1910 but the weather was too rough. Hesketh Pritchard was the author of *Sport in wildest Britain* (1921) and according to the title of his biography by Eric Parker, was a 'hunter, explorer, naturalist, cricketer'.

'The crew of the boat quietly land, the passes to the sea are blocked', wrote Hesketh Pritchard 'and a savage slaughter with clubs and staves becomes the order of the day . . . The seals are hit at the root of the nose, and the first, or at any rate the second, blow should kill. If it fails to do so, my

Cow defending her pup

Affection – as far as it goes

Bull aggrieved by rising tide

Bulls challenging

Neglected pup trying to suck an older moulted pup

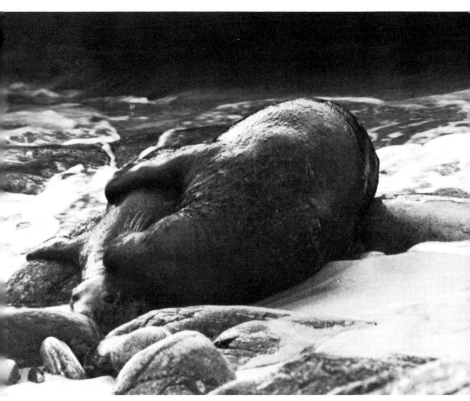

Mating at the edge of the surf

*Dunbeath Castle* at Haskeir

informants tell me that the skin swells up with suffused blood, and one might as well hit an india-rubber ball with the club for all the injury that can be done after the appearance of the swelling'.

But it was an article of Hesketh Pritchard's in the *Cornhill Magazine* of 1913 that finally inspired *An Act for the better Protection of the Grey Seal*, passed in the following year.

Protection has never since lapsed and the subsequent Act of 1932 extended the close season from 1 September to 31 December. Seal killing has gradually become casual and intermittent, whether in or out of the close season. Since the last war fishery cruisers have put in occasional appearances at Haskeir and Gasker. Summaries of the Act have appeared from time to time pinned up in island post offices. It might be wondered how protection could be more than nominal, with one policeman for Harris and another for North Uist. One answer is that in such communities the power of gossip is great and far reaching. I was told an old story of the Lochmaddy policeman whom gossip led to an old man supposed to have killed a seal. Slyly the policeman began by begging a bottle of seal oil for his ailing daughter. But then he overstepped himself and asked to see the gun; the old man replied that he had found the seal lying dead on the shore. There was no prosecution. The policeman's trick was considered to have been very mean.

The very next day after my autumn week on Shillay a Berneray lobsterman shot three seals there, for lobster bait. (No wonder the seals stampeded at the approach of a boat.) I was of course suspected of telling on him, though I knew nothing of it at the time; it was local tale telling that brought the Lochmaddy policeman.

Disuse of seal products as much as protection has aided the seals' cause and they have gone from strength to strength, founding new colonies and ever increasing the old. Haskeir has hardly shared in the general benefit; perhaps the area is too constricted and landing places are easier elsewhere. Estimates of the numbers by passing fishery cruisers – sometimes putting a party ashore – have not exceeded a hundred and twenty adults and not more than about fifty pups have been counted. Nowadays, in spite of present peace after the long and troubled past, Haskeir remains a relatively minor colony.

Elsewhere the seals have done only too well. At Coppay, Sound of Harris – the rocky islet between Shillay and Toe Head – Murdo Macdonald saw a new colony begin and grow in ten years from nil to an annual strength of a hundred pups. It is ironic that when the newly founded Nature Conservancy entered the field the problem soon became not the conservation but the control and culling of seals, now importantly called 'Management'. Culling began at the Farne Islands, then spread to Orkney and Shetland; the counts of seals killed started all over again. The Western Isles came in their turn; fisheries were being damaged, a natural resource was being denied to the inhabitants, a craft industry would aid unemployment. Permits were issued for the killing of month-old pups on Gasker, Shillay and in the new colony on Coppay. The skins were for making up into various trinkets for sale to tourists and indeed a small craft industry, aided and abetted by the Highlands and Islands Development Board, has come to flourish. Little toy seals made of real sealskin became best sellers; it seems a reflection on our times that no better use could be found for those little barrel-shaped bodies.

The culls began at Gasker and Coppay in 1966, and thereafter bad weather has as often as not prevented any cull at all. No permits were issued in either 1969 or 1970 but even when issued the allotments have seldom been taken up in full. Shillay's turn did not come until 1972, when 70 pups were culled out of a permitted 240 for the three islands, and Shillay's 70 made the total for the year.

And so the wheel has turned full circle, from hunting round to culling, from illegal clubbing to approved shooting.

At first sight the history of Haskeir seals is puzzling. Why should so difficult a rock, so often protected by wild weather, have been so foremost a hunting ground, so prominent in the records? The seals even had a local Gaelic name, *Ròn Haisgeir*.

The reasons must be several: first the traditional possession of the rights of the rock by North Uist, then the topography of the place which aided the hunters – the breeding ground elevated a hundred feet above the sea, the few constricted and easily guarded passes to and from the sea – and finally the seals themselves: they had nowhere else to go. They had little alternative but to hang on and obstinately return year after year.

Throughout the centuries of hunting there is the sense of seals always waiting offshore, in check, wanting only a sanctuary; like all life, wanting only to further their own cause. But islands sufficiently isolated for seals have always been few enough and fewer still in the past when human habitation was spread more widely. At St Kilda seals were confined to a few inaccessible caves. It was many years after the evacuation before the first seals began tentatively to haul out on the shore of Village Bay. At the Flannan Isles the cliffs always denied any access. At North Rona habitation may have kept the seals at bay for the best part of a thousand years, leaving them only a few caves and skerries. Evidently their fortunes have ebbed and flowed throughout historical times and only in very recent years have they regained an ancient inheritance.

The island names Rona and Shillay in themselves suggest some clue to seal history. There are three sizeable islands of the name Rona or Ronay in the Hebrides: North Rona, South Rona next to Raasay, and Ronay on the east side of Benbecula. There is also Eilean nan Ron, off Oronsay, where seals have a strong colony and there are various seal rocks, Sgeir nan Ron, scattered about Western Scotland. The name Rona is traditionally derived from the Gaelic word for seal, *ròn*, though it is now held that a likelier origin for the island name is in the Norse words *hraun*, meaning rough or rugged ground, and *-ey*, island. But Rona, for all its remoteness and savage climate, is not rough, nor was it discovered by the Norsemen. To an approaching ship the island rises from the sea as a smooth down, and much of the interior is quite a gentle place of soft grassy slopes. South Rona is a different matter. Its four mile long skyline is as saw-toothed as the spine of a traditional dragon and its interior is all broken cliffy slopes and boulders, and heather and scrub. The smaller Ronay by Benbecula is similarly precipitous within; *hraun* would do well enough for both of them and ancient seal colonies need not be sought at either.

North Rona may well have been discovered by seafaring monks from Iona, voyaging in search of hermitage, perhaps during the seventh century. St Ronan himself is the traditional first inhabitant – 'in this Ronay are two little cheapels where sanct Ronan lived all his tym as a heremit' – and though eremitical monks may at first have shared the island with seals it is inconceivable that a breeding colony can have survived the following centuries of permanent settlement. The seals have no alternative but to haul out on to rocks and grass where a child could walk. Neither Donald Monro nor Martin even mentioned seals at Rona or Sula Sgeir. The 'simple people' of Rona had a boat in Martin's time; whether they raided Sula Sgeir nine miles away is impossible to say; the records are silent. Seals evidently continued to frequent Rona; a tradition dating back to the early seventeenth century recalled that all the six male inhabitants of the island were drowned in Geodh Halhar while on a 'seal excursion' and at a later time part of the rent was paid in seal oil.

Habitation of Rona, tenuous enough during the early nineteenth century, finally ended in 1844 when the last shepherd, Donald M'Leod, 'King of Rona', returned to Lewis; and the seals were able at last to re-colonize their ancient quarters.

Captain Barnaby RE, who conducted the Ordnance Survey of Rona, wrote in a communication dated 1852 that seals were 'very numerous here, but not easily killed'. This of course referred to summertime. By the 1880's sealskins from Rona and Sula Sgeir were being traded in Stornoway, the hunters being fishermen out in open boats from Ness at the northern end of Lewis. Both Harvie-Brown and R. M. Barrington, another nineteenth century naturalist and yachtsman, tried to get reliable figures but 'the seal statistics are most unsatisfactory'. Evidently the numbers were substantial: in 1882, thirty from Sula Sgeir alone; in 1883, 107 from Rona. The famous two shepherds of Ness, Murdoch Mackay and Malcolm MacDonald, who exiled themselves to Rona in 1884 after a religious dispute and who died there the following year, were reported to have spent their time 'building sheep fanks, fishing, and killing seals'.

These old voyages to Rona are still within family memories; going to Rona for sealskins in October was far worse than the August trip to Sula Sgeir for the *gugas*, those unsavoury, salted down fledgling gannets. 'Once the men, running short of food, had to live on cormorant soup thickened with a little oatmeal'. When eventually they got back they did not know whether they had reached Port of Ness or Skigersta. 'It was rough and dark. The flares they had were two burning peats held to the wind. One of the men shouted "Is there anybody in Port", and his wife in Lionel sitting milking the cow, said if her husband was living that was his voice.' But the most vivid picture recalled by the listener to this tale was of the 'hardy bearded Niseachs turning away and leaving in safety a mother seal who would rather die than leave off feeding her baby and who implored them with tears running down her black velvet cheeks to move on'.

In 1905 a crew of nine men became stormbound on Rona. Twice a fishery cruiser was sent to the island but only at the second attempt was able to land provisions; the men were still in good health but 'as they had used up all the peats brought with them from home the only materials they had for fire were the skins and oil of seals they had killed'. (*Stornoway Gazette*.)

'With great difficulty the fishermen got their boat launched off the rocks and safely cleared the shore, bringing with them the skins of 180 seals. They had killed altogether over 200, but had used some of the skins, as stated, to keep their fire alight . . .'

Now some two and a half thousand pups are born on Rona every year, and the number goes on increasing.

The name Shillay – Sellay in old spelling – can be derived from the Norse word for seal, *selr*, which with the suffix *-ey* makes seal island; and which would be written in Gaelic as *seileidh*. The inference is that when Norse settlers found an island of seals, they named it as such, just as they named the various Pabbays, found to be inhabited by monks. It has even been suggested that the name Viking is associated with another word for seal, *vikan*, because the Norsemen were expert seal hunters; but this seems far-fetched.

But what about the existing inhabitants whom the Norsemen joined or replaced? They must have been poor seamen or very thin on the ground; Johannes Brøndsted* even suggested that they did not exist. 'There is archaeological evidence for the belief that, when the Viking raids began, these islands (Shetland, Orkney, Hebrides) were already, to some extent, occupied by Norwegians who had found them virtually uninhabited.'

As well as the Sound of Harris and the Monach Shillays there is, in the entrance to Loch Skiport, South Uist, a pair of Shillays, More and Beg, joined by a drying reef. Since they are unlikely sites for grey seals the etymology may fall down here unless conceivably the islands were once a centre for common seals.

The seals of the Monach Shillay must soon have been driven away – it is too near and easy a place. Even in Martin's time the purse netting he described was 'formerly' and there is no reason to suppose that any such netting would have been pursued during the breeding season.

Nor can any original colony at Shillay, Sound of Harris, have survived for long; and when boats were going regularly to Haskeir and Gasker it is impossible to believe that any colony could have been either overlooked or spared. And the grazing of Shillay was well known: 'extraordinary pasturage for sheep', said Martin, sheep with 'the biggest horns that ever I saw'.

The lack of any evidence of human habitation on

* *The Vikings* by Johannes Brøndsted (Penguin Books Ltd, 1960)

Shillay – no trace of even a shieling or ancient peat cutting – remains a puzzle. So does the re-establishment of any original seal colony. Whenever I asked along the Harris shore or in Berneray I was always told that there had been seals on Shillay for as long as anyone could remember. An elderly lobsterman in Berneray told me he remembered men going sealing to Shillay in his boyhood; this would have been about 1900. The Ordnance Survey of the island took place in 1878 and though the six inch map includes only one place name, it is a significant one: *Ard an Laoigh*, The Promontory of the Calf, or, if misspelt and properly *Laogh*, then The Promontory of the Calves. Calf can be cow's calf or seal calf. Since the promontory in question is the southern corner of a bare rock at the south-west end of the island and is separated from main Shillay by a deep gully, interpretation must point to seals. But Harvie-Brown, who first saw the Sound of Harris from the deck of the brand new s.s. *Dunara Castle* on her way to St Kilda in 1879*, never mentioned seals on Shillay. He knew the Sound well during the 1880's and once landed on Shillay; and he was well in touch with local men. There were grey seals in the Sound, but not many; 'Mr John MacDonald pointed out to him various favourite rocks in the Sound which the grey seal frequents in small numbers.' There was a well known one called *Sgeir-nam-Tapbhaist* still frequented by 'a pair'; Harvie-Brown himself saw two seals there, '*very large* and *extremely* hoary in colour'. The rock was 'out of gun – or almost rifle-shot – of any other rocks in the Sound, and the seals rest and breed in security, the young having been found, even of late years, by Mr MacDonald of Newton'. But that was all.

I took my questions to Norman Macleod of Leverburgh, an old man renowned for local legend. He agreed that Shillay had never been inhabited; peat had never been cut there, that was a clear sign. And the grazing was so good (but not so much as a shieling went with it). There wouldn't have been

* I cannot help mentioning that the *Dunara Castle* was not broken up until 1948, at Port Glasgow, where I sadly photographed her; and that I first went to St Kilda in her in 1938.

enough water in the summer (no worse than other islands).
The island could only support two or three families, that
wasn't enough to pull up a boat (but islanders often had no
boat). In fact no good reason appeared why Shillay should
not have been inhabited, in times when other and less
favoured little islands were.

There had always been seals on Shillay right enough, said
Mr Macleod, an old poetess had a song about them in the
Gaelic; she was called Mary Macleod and she was in her
nineties by the time Martin was about here, and she lived to
105. But unfortunately the sole evidence lay in her lines:

> As I sat above a seal-haunted strait,
> Looking towards Hirt of blue birds . . .

Then why didn't Martin mention the seals if they were
there? 'Och,' I was told, 'the local men wouldn't have told
him about that, they had such bad weather, and in June there
would be no seals there – they wouldn't want to talk about
such things.' (But that was just the sort of thing that Martin
was told about, and then re-told.) Dean Monro had no mention of Shillay; he was at Rodel (Roadill) with its 'ane
monasterie'; of course he would have walked along to the
Obbe ('ane water with ane gude tak of salmond fische in it'),
he would have gone on to see the old 'teampull' below
Chaipaval ('ane heich grene hill callit Copefeall'). Un-
consciously, Norman Macleod was walking with the Dean.
He brought to his texts and legends just the same literal interpretation which characterizes the persistent bible reading
of the Outer Isles.

In the old days of a self-sufficient economy every scrap of
natural product of sea, shore or land found a use. W. Ander-
son Smith, who lived with the crofters of Lewis for a time,
reeled off a list of some of them in his *Lewsiana or Life in the
Outer Hebrides* (1875). No sort of fish came amiss, not even
dogfish, and limpets and other shellfish were always a standby.
Various seaweeds were eaten – dulse; the peeled stalks of
tangle ('like a hard turnip'); caragean and a dark ware called

*slochgan*. Black oil from fish livers helped in manipulating wool when it was being spun into yarn. The dyes were *crotal*, the lichen from the rocks, for brown; water lily roots from the lochans for black; heather for yellow and soot scraped from the iron pot suspender for maroon. The roots of cinquefoil, common on the moors, were used for barking nets and lines. Fish liver oil was the fuel for the iron lamp; the wick was the pith of a rush stem. Woven rushes made grain bags for the water mill; willow wands were woven into creels. And all the seabirds and seals naturally belonged to the economy wherever they could be got.

Even in modern times seal oil – *Ola-an-Ròin* – retained something of its old magic. Roddy, an elderly man, a lobsterman friend in Berneray, told me that he'd sent bottles of seal oil as far afield as Vancouver. (It was rather like the unsavoury parcels of *gugas* from Sula Sgeir, posted to exiled Nessmen all over the world.) The blubber was boiled down in a water jacket; the oil was strained, lightly salted and bottled; then it kept indefinitely and was very nasty to take. In Berneray seal oil was still a valued medicine, though more as a preventative than as a cure – take a spoonful now and then as winter comes on. It was good for chest coughs and for tuberculosis, once the scourge of the Outer Isles. Apparent cures of T.B. were even ascribed to it; evidently it was an effective placebo, if no more.

Kenneth Macdonald, lobsterman, of Loch Roag, Lewis, told me that a friend of his father's rendered seal blubber. He took the oil neat, by the cupful, and offered it to all and sundry. This time it was a cure for rheumatism.

John Morrison, Motor Hirer, of Northton, Harris, said it was an acquired taste, but people took a fancy for it. It was better than modern fish liver oils; it had vitamins in it and the like of that. The boiled blubber yielded grades of train oil and the finest grades, strained and boiled and boiled and strained, were clear as water. It was good for asthma. The lower grades made cattle medicine, mixed with potatoes or oatmeal and given as a mash in wintertime; it was to put a bloom on their coats, or to open their bowels. And Roddy of Berneray said that raw blubber was a winter cattle medicine. You forced a lump in at the side of the cow's mouth, then held her muzzle until she swallowed.

Seal oil sometimes doubled for fish oil, as in lamp fuel or in the working of wool. Dr P. J. Macleod, who was born in Lewis, remembered the oil being used as a lubricant in the carding of wool, to prevent breakage of the staple.

John Morrison well remembered his grandfather's sealskin tobacco pouch. All the old men had them, made from a strip of hide with a pocket sewn in at one end; and the spring of the hide was such that the opened pouch rolled itself up again. There was no use for seal meat. Occasionally a hide might be used as a rug but the price of skins was too low to make hunting profitable, at any rate in his grandfather's time.

Roddy of Berneray had clubbed three moulted pups at Shillay the previous autumn, had cut up the meat into chunks and put it into barrels of brine, for lobster bait. This was worthwhile when a barrel of salt mackerel from Stornoway cost between three and four pounds and lasted only a week. And, in spite of protection, he'd had enquiries for uncured fresh hides from a Glasgow merchant.

In older days the use of seal products was wider, though Martin made no mention of seal oil. It was a Uist export, presumably as train oil, in the mid-eighteenth century, as the Reverend Kenneth Macaulay reported. He, because of landing at Haskeir, was naturally told about this by his crew. By then seal meat was no longer eaten and Martin was at pains to point out that, in his day, it was used only by the vulgar. The seals from Causamul were then salted down in the ashes of burnt seaweed and eaten in the springtime 'with a long pointed stick instead of a fork, to prevent the strong smell which their hands would otherwise have for several hours after'. The meat was astringent and cured diarrhoea and dysentery; dried liver pulverized and mixed with milk, aquavitae or red wine was good for fluxes; the flesh and broth of fresh young seals was pectoral. In North Uist a girdle of sealskin worn about the middle removed sciatica;

long strips of sealskin served as ploughing harness, instead of ropes.

The use of seal meat in the southward Catholic isles brought forth one of Martin's most splendid passages.

'THE *Seal*', he wrote, 'tho' esteemed fit only for the Vulgar, is also eaten by Persons of Distinction, tho' under a different Name, to wit, *Hamm*; this I have been assur'd of by good hands, and thus we see that the generality of Men are as much led by fancy as judgment in their Palates as well as in other things. The Popish Vulgar in the Islands Southward from this, eat these *Seals* in Lent instead of Fish, this occasion'd a debate between a *Protestant* Gentleman and a *Papist* of my Acquaintance, the former alledged that the other had transgressed the Rules of his Church, by eating Flesh in Lent, the latter answer'd, that he did not, for says he I have eat a Sea Creature, which only lives and feeds upon Fish, the *Protestant* reply'd, that this Creature is Amphibious, lies, creeps, eats, sleeps, and so spends much of its time on Land, which no Fish can do and live. It hath also another faculty that no Fish has, that is, it breaks Wind backward so loudly, that one may hear it at a great distance; but the Papist still maintain'd that he must believe it to be Fish till such time as the Pope and his Priests decide the question.'

# SEVEN

◆

# Shillay and the Seals

## I

The *Heather* lay off the beach of Shillay, rolling uncomfortably in the broken sea and snatching at her anchor cable. It had rained all day yesterday and was raining all day today, but we could wait no longer. This was the old boat's first call at Shillay; three years had gone by since my short autumnal stay on the island in 1947 and I had not been back in the interval. On this dreary afternoon in mid-July we had come for me to refresh memories and to choose the likeliest site for a long-standing camp; the coming autumn would bring me the first and the last chance for a proper residence through the seals' season.

On the way out the main channel was stained with peat from the steady rush of rain water from the land. We cleared the beacons and passed the familiar dangers – Sgeir Innes showing an ugly tooth, Colla Sgeir hidden somewhere beneath the waves, Girls Rock and The Irishman safely to starboard. We closed Pabbay with its pyramidal hill cut off short by the low ceiling of cloud, and headed across to Shillay.

All in front was the island, green and grey, mist-blown and sodden. Waves sluiced up the unmarked sand. The rain came down remorselessly. No seals were ashore but thirty or forty heads bobbed in the broken water round the boat, nostrils opening and shutting, big eyes as ever bright with interest. We pulled the dinghy up the beach and made footmarks across the soft wet sand. The slime on the rocks made them as slippery as ice. The mudslide was now a bright green tract of silverweed and iris with a running stream down the middle, overflowing from one clean pool to the next. One item I would not need to bring would be water; last time, not knowing the resources, I'd included a jerrican of drinkable water.

The obvious place for a camp was somewhere eastward and down wind of beach and mudslide, but all the hillside was oozing and anything like level ground lay in standing water. Down by the rocks was the best place but too near the seal ground, so it had to be further back and up the hill, on ground both sodden and sloping. At least there was a good view and all the rough hillside was dotted with heath orchids in fresh flower. A few dull gulls were flying about. Useful driftwood seemed to be very scanty and the two or three enormous baulks stranded at the head of the beach were far too big to move. We collected some small bits and dropped them in a heap to mark the place, and did not linger. The seals attended our going with curiosity undiminished. Soon the beach had sunk to a white strip and when that was gone the island was again a drab silhouette.

After our summer cruise and back at home I began to collect equipment. I bought an ex-Army bell tent, a dark brown tanned one, and put it up in the garden. It seemed all right, though rather dark inside. I made up a set of three storm guys, each with an eye at one end to drop over the peak of the tent. I included the essential heavy rickcloth, for covering stores or for come what might. Another piece of government surplus was a vast fourteen-inch lens, for long range photography, and when this was mounted on the front of an ancient wooden reflex camera and the whole outfit screwed on to a plank, I felt I ought to be setting off for the Crimean War. All the dry and tinned provisions I collected at home. Once again Leslie and Margaret Lomas had generously offered the hospitality of Kyles Lodge; the same back room as

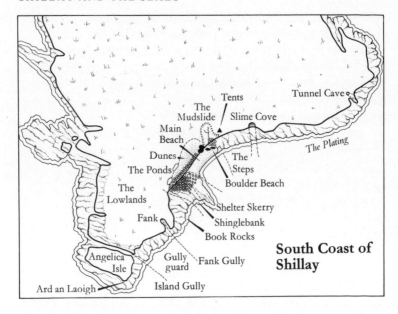

Tents

Tunnel Cave

The Mudslide

Slime Cove

Main Beach

The Plating

Dunes

The Steps

The Ponds

Boulder Beach

The Lowlands

Shelter Skerry

Fank

Shinglebank

Book Rocks

**South Coast of Shillay**

Angelica Isle

Gully guard

Fank Gully

Ard an Laoigh

Island Gully

before was ready for whatever might arrive. Murdo Macdonald had agreed to do the ferrying again.

Gradually the pile of gear and provisions accumulated until the day came to load it all into the old van. That flattened the springs and, on a trial run, the least bump brought tyres and mudguards into conflict, and the propeller shaft clattered against its tunnel. I cut away part of the offending tunnel but had to abandon some of the tinned food. A tiny cubicle was left for the driver. I filled up the engine with heavy tractor oil and set off next morning, very gingerly indeed.

All the first day the windscreen wiper kept up its mesmeric beat. A nasty hernia developed on one of the back tyres and at dusk, just as I was turning into a garage, it went off like a gunshot. But I got as far as Kendal and stopped at the first lit-up lodging that appeared, a small temperance hotel which seemed to consist entirely of stairs and corridors.

Scotland was even wetter than England. All the hills were marked with white streaks where torrents leapt out of their gullies. I reached Spean Bridge Hotel and was lucky to get the use of a divan in the private lounge. The third day behind the 'screen wiper, at an average speed of 17 m.p.h., got me to Kyle of Lochalsh but the little deck space on the *Lochmor* for Tarbert, Harris, was already booked so I had to go via Stornoway, in the *Loch Seaforth*, a detour of 70 miles by sea and 40 by land.

I left Stornoway in the evening. All went well, southing through Lewis in the dark, up and over the Clisham and down into Harris, through Tarbert and on along the rough track down the west coast. A squall cleared the salt smears from the windscreen and the stars came out. The central ridge in the road kept catching the bottom of the car with a loud clout. I went on gently, peering through the clear washed arc and following the little pool of illumination cast ahead. I would still be at Kyles by midnight. But the road was so bumpy and I was changing gear so frequently, I thought the gear lever must have jumped out; I pushed it in again, changing down, but nothing happened. The car rolled to a halt. I tried each gear in turn without response. I left the engine running and in gear, and explored underneath by torchlight: the propeller shaft was turning. So something must have failed in the back axle.

There were telegraph poles alongside the road but no sign of habitation. I tried until exhausted to shove the car over a little rise ahead so I could coast down the other side and find a place to get off the road, but it was useless and I succeeded only in breaking the glass in one of the rear windows. Not knowing what more to do, I did nothing except turn off the lights. One could have broken down in many a worse place. After a while I delved deeply into my luggage to extract a couple of blankets and then, at half past two, realizing that nothing was going to happen and I couldn't make anything happen, I curled up in the front seat and slept, this way and that. Down came the rain again.

In daylight the rain was still streaming down and splashing in the road. Tawny moorland and grey rocks stretched away on either side. The sea lay in front, with part of a large dim island in sight; that must be Taransay. The road ahead dipped in and out of sight, finally disappearing round a hillside.

Before very long a red bus appeared on the horizon, approaching and getting larger at each reappearance. It turned out to be a well-worn fifteen-seater, empty except for the driver. As I was blocking the road, he stopped. I asked for help with a shove but the car was immovable. He'd give me a lift to Leverburgh right enough, said the driver, but he was a wee bit pressed for time; 'better get the load out first', he said. So that was the easy solution and the whole lot, boxes and bags, loose blankets and all, was soon transferred in the rain and heaped up in the back of the bus. He said he'd be back in a few minutes and that he was only going on to Scarista (wherever that was). Somehow he managed to squeeze the bus past me, practically taking to the moor, and when he came back his solitary passenger was a small child. He stopped only to fill up the radiator with a bully beef tin from a nearby burn, while I threw in my last bits of luggage, and on we went.

Business was soon brisk: various waiting oilskinned figures climbed in, each saying 'terrible weather' in his turn; wet parcels were dropped at the roadside or picked up; an increasing number of children joined in; this was the school bus on its morning round. The bus clattered and bounced along the road which now followed the edge of the dunes. The Atlantic came rolling in alongside in its usual grey and white gloom. Some of the smaller children got out and stood waiting at the roadside. Some of them were barefoot, with the perfectly formed feet of children brought up shoeless. They were for the side school, I learnt, but there was no sign of any building; only the senior scholars went on to Leverburgh. Another contingent got out at another side school, this time visible, a house on the edge of the dunes with an educational globe showing through the window. Passengers got out, cheerio-ing to the driver, more got in. As my goods filled the back half of the bus, everyone had to stand up wetly wedged together. By time we arrived at the Leverburgh school only half a dozen children were left. The doors were shut; I'm afraid they were very late.

I was the only passenger while the bus started to retrace its route, turned off down the side road to Kyles Lodge, rattled over the cattle grid and swept up to the front door: late, but at least I arrived in some style. And I had difficulty in getting the driver to accept any money.

When the explanations and apologies were over – Leslie Lomas had waited up until 3 a.m. – and my goods were stacked in the back room, I went to an upstairs window and looked out across the white-flecked sea to Red Rock beacon and the battleship shape of Coppay and there, far and faint through the rain-splashed glass, lay Shillay and Little Shillay together.

The red bus was one of John Morrison's, Motor Hirer, of Northton, already a source of much friendly gossip and old memories. He made nothing of getting in the abandoned car. As usual a tattered bus was jacked up over the pit in the dark shed, its hob-nailed driver going round it with a grease gun. A bus lasted about four years, John Morrison explained, and by then each joint had worked and started the next until the whole body was 'chust a concertina', and beyond repair. The erstwhile bus was then cut down into a lorry which thereafter appeared to last for ever and ever. He recovered my car in the evening; one of the rear wheel bearings had seized up solid.

I renewed a slavish attendance on the weather forecasts. September in the Outer Isles had been a dreadful month so far and today was no better. A hard strong wind sighed in the chimneys of Kyles Lodge. The Sound was white all day and heaped up where wind and tide met. But next afternoon the sun suddenly came out and surprised crofters found themselves back at hay-making, shaking out the haycocks or turning the windrows, or even mowing. The oat harvest was the same, some uncut and mostly flattened, some cut and lying wet, some stooked in the tiny fields, some safely stacked and roped in neat cones. 'Owing to wet and stormy weather', reported the Harris correspondent of the *Stornoway Gazette*, 'it is now feared that some of the oat crop will be lost. As it is,

105

it has suffered much damage, and early hay lying out is also in a bad state.'

The evening fell to a deceptive flat calm, the Sound like a millpond, the full tide brimming against the rocks, blue peat smoke hanging in the air. But the halo'ed setting sun foretold another bout of wind and rain. That lasted for two days, then the wind turned northerly and the night sky brought a foretaste of winter; aurora borealis was alight. The vertical searchlights illuminated a bank of cloud while the sky above was starlit; the ghostly lights moved to and fro, and switched on and off as if there was someone there – like the sudden knock of a gale at the window.

I had a few more preparations to make and provisions to get. I was looking for company on the island and wanted a puppy or perhaps a kitten to come with me. One of the Northton crofts provided a sack of potatoes, so clean and white they looked as if they'd been grown in pure sand – as indeed they had. Eggs were hard to come by but we did succeed in tracking down a puppy to one of the Leverburgh crofts. It was a five-weeks old black and tan, scratching incessantly but very plump from being the only one kept out of a litter of six. Brought into the kitchen he made only a poor attempt at lapping milk. Of course he was much too young, but I had to have him and bought him for ten shillings. If I hadn't he would only have grown up untrained, barking and snapping alongside every passing car, pulling out the entrails of dead sheep and being altogether vile, like the generality of Hebridean dogs. At once his name was Shilly and Mrs Lomas took charge of him.

On only the fourth morning after my arrival – September 26, and the day I got the puppy – Murdo Macdonald called at Kyles jetty in the *Bluebell* on his way home from lobstering. It was quiet and dry under a high grey sky; the swell was easing down fast. 'If we don't try it today,' said Murdo, 'it won't be for a week; it'll be dry today but there's plenty of wind and rain to come, with the wind backing from north into west or south-west.' We settled for early afternoon. Once or twice the Kyles anemometer nearly stopped turning.

Margaret Lomas supplied last minute puppy equipment, a grocery box and an old blanket for a bed, a bottle of milk, three tins of baby food, a bowl and a tin plate. And there were presents for me, six eggs to make up the dozen, tomatoes, cake, bannocks, oranges. We were just finishing carting all the gear down to the jetty as Murdo came in sight, this time in his other boat, a recently acquired big white launch with an old but immaculately kept two-cylinder Kelvin. He had two of a crew with him, his mate and an old man with no English. It was low water and the jetty was dried out, so he had to anchor off. Everything was loaded by his small dinghy, hauled to and fro a good many times by a length of rope from the lobster creels. The last load was Leslie Lomas, myself and the puppy.

We were off just after two o'clock and Murdo was soon showing off his local knowledge by scraping alongside the rocks to keep out of the full strength of the new flood tide. For once Colla Sgeir was uncovered, a pinnacle rock surrounded by turbid shoal water. There was just enough spray coming on board to need a tarpaulin over the load; the puppy was seasick.

A boat was working lobster creels close inshore at Shillay, the *Industrious*, one of the Berneray boats. Evidently her activities had cleared any seals from the shore but it was still early in the season for them. Only a few white dots of pups showed up on the beach and on the green beyond, and inshore the lobster boat's lines of bobbing corks seemed thicker than seals' heads. At this season a boat would sink and lift her creels in one day's work. Two hours on the bottom was enough for each creel and the only advantage, in sheltered waters, of leaving them down overnight was the greater number of creels a boat could work.

To land as near as possible to the camp site Murdo first tried the rocks westward from the beach. He put out a stern anchor and eased the boat in, but there was too much lift and fall and the state of tide was awkward, so it had to be the beach. The first load was tent gear, as soon as the lines had been rigged to pull the dinghy to and fro. I set off humping the hefty sackful of bell tent. A day old pup lay dead at the head of the beach, eyeless and bloody-headed, the sand all around marked with gulls' footprints. Going on past mudslide and boulder beach I saw that all the dozen or so pups were under a week old; I was in good time. The hillside looked different, it was all sere and brown and I couldn't find the site we'd picked in July. The heap of driftwood that marked the place had disappeared. I cast about but nothing looked quite right and all the ground was squelchy. But I had to have a home, and quickly, so I chose the least sloping pitch – perhaps it was the July site after all.

The tent pegs went in all too easily, while Leslie Lomas held the pole upright, but there was a good thickness of turf and tough roots above the spongy black earth. Murdo and his mate went on unloading, hauling the dinghy up the beach with a run before the waves could break into her stern, and everything came safely ashore with no more than a few splashes. The old man with no English stayed on board. And then, when it was all in a heap at the head of the beach they kindly helped tote it along to the tent; we each in turn jumped when a pup unexpectedly snarled and snapped.

We all went back to the beach. Murdo offered me the loan of his dinghy but I thought I'd be better without it. He said he'd try and look in on me in a fortnight's time or there-abouts, and off they went. The *Industrious* had already finished and gone. She never re-appeared and nor did any other boat.

There was plenty to do before darkness. I pitched the small ridge tent down by the rocks, with its entrance facing east and a big boulder laid on each corner of its sewn-in groundsheet. At present the little tent was in reserve or for stores. But the bell tent, of necessity downwind of the seal ground, had to face south-westwards and thus look straight into the eye of the prevailing wind; I was determined to have a view of seals and coast and beach from my door. At least the Atlantic was out of sight. The Lowlands and the foot of the hill would give some slight shelter from westerly winds, the hill itself gave protection from north-west round to north-east, and winds from across the Sound, from Harris and from Pabbay, would be coming at the back of the tent.

I dug in the tent pole to bring the eaves close to the ground, and canted it so that the south-westerly eves were closest. This left the skirting loose; it would have to be anchored all round with boulders as soon as there was time. The tent so closely set seemed to hug the hillside like a limpet; I hoped it would be as well stuck. For the moment the storm guys were merely ornamental, secured to ordinary wooden pegs, but darkness was falling. Everything was heaped inside, I had shelter and company, and there hadn't been a drop of rain all day. And now, just as on my first evening on Shillay three years before, I had the satisfaction of seeing the seals coming ashore again. A cow came urging herself over the boulders, met her pup with a long mutual sniff, muzzle to muzzle, and flopped over on her side; the pup found the place and fed.

I set up the rickety camp bed on stones – the floor of the tent was already trodden into puddles. I lit Primus and lantern, warmed a drop of milk for the puppy and tried him with baby's broth, but he managed only a negligible lap. Outside I could see a single pinpoint of light from the direction of Leverburgh, ten miles away, but not a glimmer of lantern light showed through the tent.

The tent door was closely laced; the puppy was tucked up in his grocery box and so was I on the camp bed, lashed up to stop it collapsing endways. Remembered noises sounded from the outer darkness, the sea loud and near, the baby cries of pups, the wet slapping noise of a heavy cow seal climbing the rocks or the smack of a flipper beating the sea. Sometimes a stray cry was so like someone calling out that it gave me sudden gooseflesh before I had time to realise it was seal, not man.

When the wind got up in the night I could feel the ground shaking, and then came the lash of rain. I was up at three o'clock to feed the puppy. The first anxious night was hardly idyllic, nor was next morning when broad daylight brought only a brown twilight into the tent. A peep outside revealed curtains of rain driving before a rough south-wester; even

109

Pabbay was lost. Everything inside the tent was already sticky damp or dewed with moisture and in places the rain drove through as a fine mist.

Urgent work was to secure the tent as best I could and for a start that meant finding solid anchorage for the three storm guys. The stock of driftwood along the head of the beach consisted of a thirty foot tree trunk complete with the remains of its roots, an enormous baulk of fifteen inch square timber and a most useful fifteen foot length of nine by three, which at once I cut in half and dragged up to the tent. This splendid haul, sawn into shorter lengths, provided most of the posts required. For the rest there were only a few bits of driftwood to be found thrown up along the rocks, and they were mostly worm-eaten pit-props worn down to stumps. By the end of the day I had three massive bollards planted for the storm guys and a ring of eleven stumps round the tent, alternating with ordinary pegs; all the lot dug in and wedged with boulders hammered in with bigger boulders. I had time to notice the pretty devil's bit scabious scattered round the tent, still in fresh flower and with even a bedraggled bumble bee hanging on to one of them. In places there was a depth of two feet of soil above bedrock, and the post holes filled up with black water as soon as dug. I had a borrowed crowbar and found I could get some of the posts jammed into broken rock. Whatever else gave way I felt confident that the posts would not. I even became more optimistic about the tent, though the canvas tautened or slackened with disconcerting speed. Everything in the Hebrides is wind dried – hay and harvest, peat, laundry, wool – anything put out dries as soon as the rain stops. The wet tent was tight as a drum, the rain stopped, and in no time the canvas was a slatting sail.

Drinking water was surprisingly difficult, compared with the wealth of clean water in July; it might be a problem after all. All the rock pools were brackish and hillside pools ranged in colour from strong black coffee to weak tea, and smelt. I dug out a well beyond the top of the mudslide, where round leaves of pennywort showed among rank sedge and a tiny pool had formed against a rock outcrop. The turf was exceedingly tough and it took a long time even to open a small pool of black peaty mud. I left it to settle and meanwhile had to go about with a bucket, getting a mugful here and there from fairly clear puddles.

I made a start at carting and heaping boulders on the tent skirting and ended the day by going down to the beach to cut a four foot length from the enormous baulk. The little saw was barely longer than the width of the timber; at home it would hardly have seemed a practical proposition but life in the Hebrides is timeless, so I followed the custom of the country and sawed patiently away. It was gratifying when a big brown bull came back to the beach and held his ground, snapping at any pup who shuffled too near. I rolled the cut-off lump over and over all the way back to the tent, where it made a much wanted table.

During the day the puppy took properly to his food; he lapped milk and finished his baby's broth; he started chewing a soaked ship's biscuit and worried a piece of string. Mrs Lomas admitted afterwards that she hadn't expected him to survive, but once past his doubtful start he never looked back and as soon as his own supplies were used up he shared my food. But something had to be done about his incessant scratching and his skin was covered with sores. Medical stores consisted only of a carton of DDT dust and a tin of Vaseline, and this was just what was wanted. I worked the dust into his coat and treated the sores with Vaseline. The scratching ceased at once and the sores healed in a day or two.

Most of the second day went in the seemingly endless labour of carting up boulders to anchor the tent skirting and to pave half the floor. The wind rapidly freshened to gale force. A biscuit tin happened to be touching the tent – at once there was a hole in the canvas. So far I hadn't attempted any unpacking and merely snatched the easiest available food but at midday I did get the new portable wireless set, like a small attaché case, set it on my knees and opened the lid. Out came shrieks of girlish laughter – the comedian went on with his patter – it was called 'Workers' Playtime' – what an extraordinary invention – but I caught the continuing gale warning.

The gale was westerly and came in savage squalls of rain and hail between bursts of brilliant sunshine. The hail rattled against the tent like shot, I thought it must come through, and the rain was near enough horizontal to spray through the ventilators at the peak. One instant rainbow followed another; it was April supercharged. The seals on the beach lay in perfect indifference, though I did notice one shake its head after a bombardment of hail. A fiercer gust brought a sudden snowstorm of white bubbles flying past, a beautiful picture in the incandescent sunlight. This was froth blown across the island from the Atlantic side. The suds lay sparkling on the grass for minutes together before they dissolved. After another snowstorm I broke off boulder carting and went to investigate the source. Surf came pouring into a gully to be trapped at the head and there so beaten that from above it looked like thick cream. The rocks above were plastered white, the stuff stuck like paint, and now and then a cloud of froth took off and went whirling away. A smoke of spray rose above the gap between Shillay and Little Shillay and swept downwind, as if an unseen train was rushing along the cutting between the two islands. On the way back I found a couple of new pools, well above seal ground and rather less dark and smelly than the rest – good enough to solve the water supply.

The loose half of the tent skirting went on flapping wildly until at last I had it all anchored with a ton or two of boulders. I put my back against the inside of the tent to take the weight of the wind and wondered how the canvas could carry such a load. The noise and the struggle made me think it couldn't stand much more of that. A seam began to open.

This naturally was foreseen; as well as spade and crowbar I had brought a bag of cement; I had it in mind to build some sort of half-underground bothy, partly for recreation but probably of necessity as well. I roughly cobbled the seam with sacking needle and twine, and before the day was out had chosen the site for an earth house and had started work. The place was below the tents where hillside turf gave way to the beginning of coastal rock. There was a small oblong rock platform backed by a miniature cliff of earth and turf. I started to dig back the earth and stones to enlarge the platform and to make a rear wall; the front wall would have to be built up with stones along the outside edge of the platform; one end would carry round to join the rear wall, the other would be the entrance hole, facing the sea. The roof would be rickcloth on driftwood rafters. I scurried back to the tent for the worst of the squalls. Probably I could have dug out and covered some sort of shelter hole in the dunes in one day's work, but I meant to avoid disrupting the seals' lives unless absolutely necessary.

During all this activity I had half an eye for my island companions. I took my supply of boulders from the nearest top corner of the boulder beach, being both the most convenient source and least disturbing to the seals. The mudslide above was as yet hardly marked by seal tracks; the lush green silverweed of summer had curled up into white, fern-like fronds, as if scorched. A crowd of seals moved up and down the beach with the tide. The old seaman's expression, 'as wet as a half-tide rock', exactly suited them. Nothing could have been wetter than seals lying in the surf, letting the waves break over them, their hides glistening in the sun. This was the time of big spring tides. At high water there was hardly any sand left, the seals were pushed into a line among the boulders and all the sheltering rocks and skerries disappeared. I thought I recognized some big bulls from three years ago.

By the evening half the tent floor was paved with boulders and all my belongings were perched up on them, away from the sodden ground. For the time being I had to spread the rickcloth over the rest of the floor, which would otherwise have soon been trodden into mud. The gale began to ease during the night and the squalls became less frequent; the tent had survived the first attack. The puppy had me up at four o'clock in the morning. Outside the moon's full face showed among the running clouds; the time and place and unearthly

113

light were enough to send a shiver down the spine.

The morning brought a lovely flood of sunshine. Now I could turn my back on the tent and go off on a survey, leaving Shilly full, fed and asleep in his box, his puppy tummy rising and falling.

The six inch map was not much help, being no more than outlines of high and low water marks with the interior marked merely with the crescent dots of 'rough pasture'. Very well: Shillay is nearly an equilateral triangle with its apex and hilltop pointing to the north-west, and an interior of rolling downland. The north- and west-facing sides are cliffy and rockbound all along; my concern was with the third side, the base line, the seals' coast, half a mile long and slightly concave at the beach in the middle. The *West Coast Pilot* even called it 'a small bay on its south-eastern side, where landing might be effected'. One day later on I happened to be up the hill when all the island lay under a dark pall, except that one shaft of sunlight struck through the cloud and illuminated the tiny beach down below. I said to myself then, as often before and afterwards, 'Where there is sand there is hope.' The small area of beach and dunes make a little sea garden, the natural centre and the gem of Shillay.

At home I had used the six inch map to make enlarged copies of the south-eastern coast and now I went to divide it up into sections, naming them and counting pups as I went along.

The famous beach – 'Mainbeach' – is a hundred yards long and fifty yards wide between tide marks. At the head is a fringe of dry boulders and behind them miniature sand cliffs and bunkers lead into an acre or two of dunes. Sand sedge and lyme grass are the sand binders here and the dunes are an area of sweet bright green turf, with primroses in season. In a low part of the dunes and just back from the beach lay the remains of what I called 'the Bothy', but it was no more than an incomplete outline of beach boulders, and only one or two courses showed above the sand. I never found a chance to dig it out.

The eastern end of the beach is fenced in by two great

whalebacks of rock – 'the Sgeirs' – rising from the sand and separating Mainbeach from the boulder beach beyond. A narrow sand-floored gap is left between the landward end of the upper sgeir and a steep rock – 'Dune Rock' – which rises inland and disappears under the last of the dunes. The gap is just wide enough for seal or man to pass through and was a route much used by both; it is awash at high water.

The boulder beach is a stretch of large bare boulders, some forty yards in length along the turf rim at the top and twenty-five yards deep; the boulders, although so smooth, made awkward going for seals on their way to the mudslide above. The mudslide, a shallow little valley marked with pools and peaty trickles, is enclosed by Dune Rock and dunes on one side and by the fall of the hill on the other; the final trickle from it disappears under the boulders below and, at low water, reappears as shining chestnut coloured pools against the lower sgeir, and stains the surf and sea beyond. Upwards the mudslide soon merges into boggy hillside to share a water-shed with another shallow basin which falls away to level off behind the dunes. As the land falls the soggy turf gets wetter and wetter until it ends in standing water – the 'Ponds'. There are two good sized ponds, one draining into the other by a peat-walled rivulet, and easily reached by seal routes over the dunes. If not originally created by seals the ponds have evidently been enlarged by generations of wallowing. In summer they are surrounded by deep beds of docks but now all that remained was a thicket of leaning or fallen rusty sticks.

All the rest of this coast, on either side of the beaches, is rock – steep-to or gradual, solid or broken – and at high water little sense of a bay remains.

Going eastwards from the boulder beach the first feature of note is the interesting remains of some sort of rough bothy or earth house, apparently never finished, and not far above is evidence of two old camp sites, marked by heaps of boulders and driftwood, ditches and turf banks.

The stretch of coast below I called 'the Steps', because it does go down to the sea in rocky steps. There are some platforms safely above high water, but the only seal pup there when I landed was washed away in the first gale. Next comes 'Slime Cove', a little inlet floored with large boulders, slippery and green with algae – a bad place for seals with only a small area of boulders above high water and with cliffs behind. There were two pups here, one live and one dead; the dead one draped over a boulder and perhaps washed round from the Steps. It was pathetic to see the evidence of the pup's struggle for life, its flippers and chin worn down to raw flesh.

After Slime Cove comes 'the Plating', a smoother tract of rock like boiler plates, which carries right on to 'Tunnel Cave', where the coast turns the corner and meets the Atlantic swell curling round from the north side. This was getting beyond seal ground, there were only two pups along the 300 yard length of the Plating. Tunnel Cave itself has an inland blow hole, where the roar of shingle in the backwash comes up from below. Beyond Tunnel Cave and round the corner the north-facing coast runs westward for 1000 yards of unremarkable broken cliffs, indented by two geos. The first geo was always quiet and produced the singularly useless information that a boat could land there in any gale except northerly and the crew get up the rocks by easy steps. The next geo is smaller and cliff-sided.

The cliffs gather from either side to the north-west corner of the island and the highest point of land is only a little inland. There is no summit cairn. It would be proper to erect one but there are no loose stones lying up there.

The other end of the base line, from the beaches southwestwards to land's end, is backed by 'the Lowlands', a low-lying and peninsular area of some twelve acres of more or less level seaside turf, littered with rocks of all shapes and sizes, about two hundred yards across and all within easy range of storm spray.

The southward end of Mainbeach is partly sheltered by a long spur of rock – 'Shelter Skerry' – but this disappears at high water. Beyond is 'Shinglebank', under whose stones trickles the overflow from the lower pond. Then comes 'Book Rocks', where the strata are nearly vertical and look like slates on edge, some sharp, some worn – the mouldering leaves of an enormous book. Book Rocks end in 'Fank Gully', a remarkable narrow parallel-sided cleft, striking fifty yards into the land, and partly sea-floored. The strata of Book Rocks make the sides vertical, a natural jetty where a boat could lie alongside. At the head of the gully is the fank itself, a straggling enclosure of wire netting strung on posts jammed into rock crevices. The stock of sheep had been taken off here the previous June, so Simon Mackenzie, the grazier, had told me. At present the island was unstocked – only seals and self. I now realized just how flat calm the sea must be to get a boat up that little drain. A new stock of sheep would be coming out to overwinter as soon as the weather was fit, Simon Mackenzie had said, perhaps not until the end of October or even November, but fank and gully were not needed for that; they were used only for the gathering and embarking of sheep in summertime.

Beyond Fank Gully comes 'Gullyguard', an indeterminate stretch of broken rock but with an area of loose dry stones above it. The significance of these stones was not apparent until the following summer.

Gullyguard and the Lowlands come to an abrupt end at 'Island Gully', with 'Angelica Isle' on the other side. Probably the sea comes right through the gully but mostly it is hidden below a tumble of enormous boulders; the gully itself is impassable to seals and sheep but one can easily scramble across to Angelica Isle, which is a big rock lying across the end of the Lowlands and as wide, a rectangle measuring some hundred and fifty yards by sixty or seventy. Beyond again is a turbulent, rock-encumbered channel, 200 yards wide, with Little Shillay standing on the far side, black and green, and twice the height of the Lowlands.

Much of the surface of Angelica Isle is a desert of lichened bare rock but what vegetation there was at once showed the absence of grazing. The old matted grass was a thick spring mattress, now dotted with the dead stems of angelica, like little brown trees. Land's end of Angelica Isle is the Ard an Laoigh, already mentioned, The Promontory of the Calf, the single place name marked on the six inch map. It seemed more likely than ever that Angelica Isle must have been the seals' first foothold on their return to Shillay, though now it hardly counted as seal ground. Two bulls lay hopefully on the rock but during my time only four pups came to be born there.

In heavy weather, as I soon found out, Island Gully was feet deep in foam and any cleft along the Atlantic side of the Lowlands was a soapmaker. Some great storm had flung a wartime mine far above high water, as if it had been a ping-pong ball; now it lay with the outer shell rusted through but the explosive container was still intact within. All this coast is a fearful mess of sharp and broken rock, looking as if it had been blown up with high explosive; all along the crushing, splintering and splitting of solid rock is evidence of the colossal forces of an unimaginable past. At this time of year there was more colour in the lifeless rocks than on the land, and some exposures of quartz shone like ice. Professor R. F. Heddle, the geologist, included a lively account of the rocks of Shillay in Harvie-Brown's *Vertebrate Fauna of the Outer Hebrides* (1888). 'This islet', he wrote, 'is cut in two by an east and west fault. Its northern portion shows great curved red and green beds, so boldly and clearly displayed in section by the fault that it resembles a huge diagram. On account of the exalted metamorphism resulting from the crushing, the rock is throughout excessively granular and rough, whatever direction it be fractured in. The constituent minerals – nacreous red felspar, with Haughtonite – and quartz with dark hornblende – segregate apart. All is grit-like and sharp-angled. The southern portion of the islet is a mere heap of ruins; the shattered rock, here fissile, and of fine-grained structure, being tossed erect, and resembling a mass of scorched ruins.'

On this day of survey, 29 September, only twenty-four pups had yet been born, scattered in ones and twos and threes along the length of coast from the Plating to Island Gully. The only concentration was the half-dozen on the beach. No movement inland had yet started and no pup was more than ten days old. The first pup of the season would have been born about 19 September. Even the gloriously fat bulls on station were well scattered. The usual crowd of animals – bulls, cows and a few much more lively yearlings – moved up and down the beach with the tide. I soon realized that the central part of the beach was treated as a freeway to the Ponds and Lowlands and as a neutral parking place, where some of the animals were non-breeders and could lie in peace, free from territorial and parental squabbles.

There was one more quiet day before the wind and the rain came back in earnest. September rainfall measured at Kyles was twelve inches and October started as if it meant to do better than that. I looked out through the gusting sheets of rain to the wet slugs of seals on the mudslide. The rickcloth flooring of the tent lay in puddles of water and the indoor grass was a bog. As soon as the rain eased I set to digging drainage ditches, a trench all round the tent eaves for a start, with outlets leading away radially. The spade just bounced off the thick mat of turf and had to be wielded like an axe. As ponds formed in the ditch I left a dam to the last and then let go a splendid torrent. I went on to cut a deep inverted 'V' above the tent, to intercept some of the hill drainage, and by the end of a long afternoon had dug over fifty yards of ditches. By the time I had finished the place looked like a peat working, which indeed it was, for the black slabs dug out would eventually dry to make good fuel. The inverted 'V' discharged a burn at each end; they looked as if they would go on running permanently. Conditions in the tent improved at once.

Shilly already had a dog creep through the tent skirting, and now he had to be provided with a driftwood bridge over the ditch as well; his tent training was going quite well. The miniscule piddles were acceptable indoors – indeed I kept a few old tins on hand myself for the worst of the weather, and emptied them through the dog creep into the ditch outside. For the rest and in any weather I had to make an often remarkably uncomfortable visit to the seaside rocks. However, some domestic standards had to be kept up and Shilly's attachment to the rickcloth had become altogether too sordid. I hauled it out, pegged it with boulders, and sluiced it down with bucketfuls of water from rock pools. Every precious bit of driftwood I found went into the tent as a duckboard, until eventually the rickcloth could be folded up and kept in reserve for its proper purpose of emergency shelter.

Shilly set the routine each morning, and he made for early rising. He usually woke me up at about four o'clock and by seven his attentions could no longer be ignored. I pulled some dank clothes into bed to warm them up, and covered up the bed with a groundsheet as soon as I was out of it. Then, in fur-lined boots and fur-lined jacket, sitting in the chair with a mug of hot coffee and a cigarette, I was ready to face the day, while Shilly's riotous activity exhausted itself and he collapsed asleep in his box. He was blithely indifferent to the weather, his appetite grew beyond bounds, and he took to sleeping under my jacket at the foot of the bed. But his refusal to go out at night still left plenty of mess to clear up. I wouldn't have been without him for worlds.

The chair was a blessing; not a deckchair – that would have been useless – but a proper upright canvas chair borrowed from Kyles. I spent hours in it, sometimes mooning, but more often sitting in it set up at the windward corner of the tent door, while I watched the chessboard movements of seals along the beach, and perpetually wiped the rain spray from my binoculars. I had to keep more or less dry for the want of any means of drying wet clothes.

Reading a book in the tent was a very severe test for any of their authors; I had plenty of books but it is inappropriate to sit down at nine o'clock in the morning, chilled in hands and feet, with the page tilted towards a slit of light, and wet with spray. Most remained unread. How I envied my neighbours, the shepherds of Pabbay, their proper indoors and fireside! A white tent would have been a vast improvement on my dark brown cage but a hut would have been heaven. Anything would have done, anything however small, with a door and a window; a portable hen house would have been ideal. It could easily have been anchored with wire and boulders, the sections could have been floated ashore, but getting such a

The bull of Book Rocks

Peaceful scene on the mudslide, Shillay

*Overleaf:* Leverburgh, Sound of Harris, from summit of Roneval, showing part of Ensay, Pabbay, Shillay and Little Shillay

'The Orphan' steals a feed while the cow's own new-born pup searches for the teats at the back of her head

*Heather* stranded in Loch na Ban, Sound of Harris

thing up from the South would have been an unmanageably expensive proposition, and my resources were strictly limited.

My moods changed as fast as the weather. When beautiful sunshine struck through the racing clouds I wondered whether all the bad days had been true, and as soon as they came back I wondered how the sun could ever come out again. But I never wanted to get away, or to talk to anyone except to Shilly or to myself, I only wished the wind would drop.

I soon lost count of the gales and I feared and dreaded each renewal, often heralded by the ominous warning 'severe at times'; I was forever tapping the little pocket barometer; I was like a bad sailor anticipating the next ghastly voyage.

The savage weather provided its own dramas. One night, after a sudden bout of wind and rain, I looked out and saw a half circle of colourless rainbow spanning sea and land beyond the beach. It was a rainbow by moonlight. In a few minutes it was gone, the stars came out above and the moon peeped over the hill behind. On another stormy night, when the rain had broken up into squalls, I crawled outside. The clouds were banked all round, the stars clear overhead, and one great searchlight of the aurora was struck across the sky. I stood in the steady rush of wind, and saw the dim tumultuous sea. A fine night!

When the wind was at the back of the tent there was no trouble. When it blew across the front I could set the lay of the flaps accordingly, but when it came straight at the doorway there was nothing for it but to lace up; then the only way to get in and out was to wriggle along the ground, full length in the mud. Inside I kept the windward ventilators stuffed with rags. Daylight showed through holes in the canvas and the rows of pinpoints where the stitching of the seams had failed; the lantern had to be lit. It was better after dark when there was no daylight lost and the holes no longer showed. If the wind was not too strong I could get up quite a good fug indoors, with the Primus going full bore with a red hot tin lid on top, but both lantern and torch were needed to cook and eat by. Why ever hadn't I brought a proper Tilley – the universal hissing Hebridean Tilley – instead of the feeble yellow wick I had. I was perpetually attending to the guy ropes and wondering what to do for the best. In the wet the canvas was drum tight and taking a tremendous strain but that was better than the fearful slatting that started as soon as it dried. I kept the guys as tight as I dared but inevitably more seams began to open. My first repairs, with a curved sacking needle, still held, but the needle made much too big a hole and the rain streamed through. I had to turn to a smaller, straight needle: push it halfway through the canvas from inside – waiting for a momentary lull in the slatting – trot outside and round the tent, pull the needle through and push it back, trot inside, pull it through and push it back, and so on and so on and so on. Of course the lacing hooks on the doorway deliberately snatched at my clothes every time I squeezed in or out. I spent an hour or two at this ridiculous occupation and then smeared the result with the useful Vaseline. The repairs held but further sessions of 'walking sewing' came up regularly, always accompanied by the malignant snatch of the lacing hooks.

Sometimes I retired to the little tent and tried to read. Drainage ditches and a protective turf wall had already been provided but the stalwart little tent, a pre-war veteran of the Outer Isles, could no longer withstand gale-driven rain and there was generally a pool on the floor, until I cut a hole to let it out. I kept the folded rickcloth there, as a mattress above pond level, in case of a midnight disaster to the big tent.

I got out whenever I could – anything to get away from the hateful tent. I felt better when I had the idea of treating the wind as a personal enemy, an enemy to be beaten. I worked away at the earth house, welcoming the hard labour, moving great rocks inch by inch with the crowbar, trying not to care when the wind blew the coat back over my head.

The supply of angular land rocks soon ran out and I had to turn to smooth boulders from the beach to continue the outside wall; and only cement could bond such oversized marbles. A tent on Shillay was not the best of storage quarters for cement and the outside of the bag had set to a rocky crust. In the evenings I took a lump at a time, on the lid of a biscuit tin, and hammered it back into some sort of powder; at least it made a competitive noise to answer the wind, and was something to do: like Lachie Macleod, the Shepherd of Pabbay, sawing net floats in half with a broken hacksaw blade. Shilly slept on my knees meanwhile; the Hebrides continued timeless. Anywhere but here I could have sworn to children's crying, a woman singing – windblown snatches from the outer darkness.

The mortar did not look promising: knobbly cement, well salted shell sand and dark brown peaty water; acid versus alkali. The back earth wall of my house naturally delivered a rivulet on to the rock floor, in spite of a drainage ditch above. I tried to lead it off but the mortar dam washed away. Rain washed away half the mortar in the front wall before it could set – but it showed no sign of setting.

Frustration got hold of me: the weather, the indoor wet and gloom, the mortar, the hopeless slippery boulders, even the looked-for geese failed to arrive. Failure. I aimed to make a series of photographs of the growth of seal pups from birth to weaning to independence but a whole week was lost before I could even be sure of an indubitably new-born pup. It was all going wrong; last time had been an island idyll, this time was fast turning from adventure to ordeal.

But frustration was wrong-headed; the Hebridean ethos is acceptance, resignation, gaiety, not frustration. But I did want to show some result from all my efforts.

And one day there was an excitement. I had been round the north coast, heading into squalls of wind and rain, and turned homewards over the summit and down the hillside. Suddenly down below, close inshore in the bay, a big black triangle was sticking out of the water. Momentarily I wondered what extraordinary antic a seal or seals could perform to make such a silhouette. Or a basking shark? No, the great tall sail of a fin belonged to a killer whale. Then there were three more smaller fins. The school was working slowly westwards along the coast. The big one, the bull, was so close in he must have been rubbing the rocks, his fin was in broken water. Not a seal's head was to be seen. When he lazily rolled and blew, he showed his blunt nose and the white patch on his flank. They cruised slowly away, rolling and blowing.

And in a few days the cement mortar had set rock hard.

# II

It occurred to me that I was the most solitary person in all the British Isles. All the lighthouse keepers had company. Perhaps there was a lonely shepherd far up some remote glen, but he had only to walk downhill to find a fellow human being. I could always wave to a passing boat, except that no boat passed, and in distress a bonfire, if I could find enough driftwood and be lavish enough with paraffin, would surely bring some response. Not that I minded; solitude was what I was here for. I did envy the cottage comforts and security of my nearest neighbour, Lachie Macleod, nearly three miles away and out of sight on the other side of Pabbay, but I knew he had a mate along with him that year, which must have spoilt his sought-after solitude, his own fireside, his carefully rationed radio programmes.

But I found solitude disappointing. I had wondered whether isolation of itself might not vouchsafe some insight, some clarity, an escape from linear time. Lachie Macleod had second sight. Is it a faculty of race or of isolation, or of both? The Lapps of old 'undoubtedly possessed what today would be called psychic powers, for they appear to have had frequent knowledge of events which were happening at a distance . . .' wrote Olive Murray Chapman.* The classic case in the Scottish outermost isles is that of the two shepherds who exiled themselves to empty Rona in 1884, as penance after a religious dispute with their minister. It was the recurring presentiments of an old woman in Lewis that caused the relatives to sail to the island early the follwing year, to find both men lying dead. Rona seems to have been fertile ground for

* *Across Lapland with Sledge and Reindeer* by Olive Murray Chapman (Penguin Books Ltd, 1939)

clairvoyance. Towards the end of the seventeenth century Mr Daniel Morison, minister of Barvas, visited the island. 'Upon my landing [says he] the Natives receiv'd me very affection-ately; and addressed me with their usual Salutation to a Stranger, *God save you, Pilgrim, you are heartily welcome here; for we have had repeated Apparitions of your Person among us*, after the manner of the second Sight, *And we heartily congratulate your Arrival in this our remote Country.*' (Martin Martin, 1703). In 1938, when Frank Fraser Darling was on Rona to see the seals through their season, the German crisis blew up during September. He had an un-pleasant dream that the fishery cruiser was coming to take away him and his family; and next day – so it did. I myself was qualified: I had once glimpsed an unaccountable cloaked figure striding along the cliff edge of Handa Island and of old I had had undeniable though trivial previsions of scenes to be enacted the following day. But second sight traditionally deals in unhappiness and tragedy; perhaps I was better without it.

All the same, solitude was disappointing; life remained obstinately on the surface, I slid on the slimy driftwood in the tent and cursed. Damp biscuits and margarine, another burnt-out washer in the Primus. I had only a single bottle of rum and not enough cigarettes. Nothing happens unless one makes it happen. It was no good going to all the trouble of isolating oneself and then expecting something else to happen of its own accord.

Sometimes on dreary days of 'nothing much' I thought of the tinker of Haskeir – he must have found plenty of them in his time. The rock was so clear cut to the southward on any reasonable day. More often I thought of another castaway, and he was that pathetic anonymity of wartime, the Rona sailor. To be the sole survivor from a sunken ship, to have got ashore, only to find that the land was desert Rona! This is as good a place as any to tell the story of George Rona.

On 23 April, 1941, a Whitley aircraft of No. 612 Squadron took off from Wick on a practice flight over the Atlantic.

125

Wing Commander J. B. M. Wallis, commanding the squadron, was captain and pilot. For purposes of the exercise he decided to turn on Rona but as he reached the island an oil pipe fractured in the port engine. The cumbersome secret equipment under each wing made the aircraft very difficult to fly on one engine. There was a roaring east wind and a high sea; the aircraft was already losing height; in the few seconds left for a decision the captain chose to land on Rona.

He came in from the west and into a strength of wind that effectively cut his speed. He got down safely, no one was hurt, the aircraft was not badly damaged and the wireless transmitter was still working. In four hours an Air Sea Rescue launch had arrived, racing downwind from Kirkwall. The aircrew got on board, the launch lay overnight under the lee of the island, and next morning returned uneventfully to Thurso. For this part of the story I am indebted to Air Commodore Wallis himself; for the next part to Squadron Leader D. C. F. Waller who, as Flight Sergeant, was in charge of the salvage; since the aircraft and its secret equipment were to be the subject of an equally secret salvage operation.

HM Trawler *Preston North End* landed the party within a few days, and by the evening of the first day all the heavy salvage equipment, the tents, food, water, arms, W/T gear and even carrier pigeons was safely ashore and hauled up the cliff. The trawler departed – to return in four days with more water – and Waller went in search of a camp site. He found the village, 'moss-covered and almost totally disintegrated . . . somebody, sometime lived there, that was evident. But who – and when?' The village became their headquarters.

During the next fortnight the aircraft was dismantled, the sections manhandled on sledges to the cliff edge and made ready for lowering. Then a steel cableway, with a running chain hoist, had to be rigged, spanning a corner of relatively quiet water. A lighter was called for and in three days all the sections, each of about one ton weight, were safely loaded. The whole operation was completed just within one month of the crash landing. This remarkable feat would make a story in itself; and the aircraft flew again.

Flight Sergeant Waller threw out a few asides. Once, when weather prevented the trawler from coming with supplies, they fried gulls' eggs and ate them 'with gusto and without detrimental result'. Their camp was in the village ruins; 'it was whilst exploring these in an endeavour to satisfy our curiosity we found the mummified remains of a human being. Except for a few mouldering scraps of clothing there was no means of identification, we could only assume that he was a seafaring man who had made the island after his ship had been torpedoed. Had crawled into the shelter of the ruins and died of starvation or exhaustion, possibly both. This was reported to the Naval Authorities but when I left after my stay of twenty days his blackened remains still lay curled in a cranny in the stonework'.

The version of this that got back to the Whitley's aircrew was that the salvage party had found a skeleton by the summit cairn on Toa Rona and had buried it there under the name of George Rona. Another rumour, current in Stornoway, was that a trawler had been sent, either to bring back the remains or to give them a Christian burial. The truth must have been as Waller stated, that this poor man had had the strength to roam the island, to find the village and to find shelter there; and no more. He had better died at sea.

The first cruise of the re-furbished, post-war *Heather* took her to Rona, at the end of July 1946. Of course we were looking for relics but no single bit or piece of aircraft was to be found, nor even a scar in the turf, nor any human trace in the village. The usual nestling fulmars squatted in the corners of St Ronan's cell, the village lay under its summer mantle of wet grass and weeds, pervaded by the smell of Leach's petrels. It was a rushed visit; the weather was worsening and we had to go.

In 1952 the naturalists Mr and Mrs Lauder Smith (Rosemary Studdy) spent a week on Rona. One night they were looking for petrels in a bothy and found by torchlight a human skull, lying in a crevice in the wall. They buried it under the turf of the graveyard wall.

Some years later Dr Robert Morrison, who knew Rona

from visits in his yacht *Mary Rose of Morar*, gave a stranger a lift in his car. Coincidence now reached out a very long arm: his passenger turned out to have been a member of the 1941 salvage party, and he pitched Dr Morrison a very tall yarn (which later found its way into the *Stornoway Gazette*): 'When the wind changed after they had been in camp for a night or two [said the stranger] they were disturbed by a powerful stench. When they investigated, expecting to find a dead sheep, they found the body of a German naval officer, propped against the wall of a bothy, in his No. 1 uniform and wearing his hat. There was no identity disc or papers as one would expect to find if he had tried to live there, and yet, if he had been shipwrecked, how did he have his hat?'

In 1958 Mr and Mrs Lauder Smith were again on Rona, this time with the Glasgow University Expedition of that summer. The place where they had buried the skull was bare of turf and the skull was gone.

For all the peace the poor man has had he might as well have left his bones to an anatomy school.

England in early October was enjoying a spell of settled summery weather with temperatures rising to 70°F., so the wireless said. This was hard to believe on Shillay. The gale of 3 October was rated very severe; all the afternoon (at Kyles) the wind speed stayed over 50 m.p.h. and an inch and a half of rain went with it. But at least it was southerly and came across the Sound to Shillay. The storm of the 7th was much worse, and westerly; it woke me at three in the morning with a cannonade of rain and after that there was too much noise to sleep through. When we got up at seven o'clock for the weather forecast I said to Shilly, 'What do you think the barometer's doing this morning, I expect the bottom's dropped out of the bloody thing.' So it had, in effect. This was the customary 'very deep depression off north-west Scotland, moving eastwards'.

When I struggled outside I could hardly stand. Shilly ventured forth, faithfully trying to maintain his tent training, but he was promptly blown over and crawled back indoors on his belly. My own visit to the seaside rocks was of unprecedented discomfort. I tried to read a book but without success, I tried the little tent but it was no better. I wondered how one of the native men would have managed the circumstances, with their well-known facility for doing nothing satisfactorily. Not like me, I was sure; it was all very well doing nothing in quiet weather – but now! For me it was a wretched state of anxiety: insides turned to water, a racing heart beat when the squalls struck, an undercurrent of fear for the gunshot explosion that would burst the tent to shreds.

I got out and crouched by the earth house, trying to think clearly in the tearing wind full of spray and sand. Suds from the boulder beach came snowstorming past. The front wall of rounded boulders could go no higher and the earth wall at the back was not high enough; I should have to build up some sort of wooden framework on top. I turned to and dug out a hole for a timber upright. A cow seal working up the mudslide was plastered white with blown sand. The whole beach was veiled in blowing sand. What sort of a refuge would be a pit dug in the dunes?

The sea was sand-coloured far out into the Sound of Shillay, huge seas were breaking along the coast of Pabbay on the other side and masked the land where it fines down to a long shallow point. Spray like storm clouds rose high over Little Shillay – like the plume from a depth charge hanging momentarily before being swept into oblivion. Time and again a great grey-white cloud rose from behind the islet, and paused, and vanished. All the lowlands were lost in spray.

'Severe at times today' said the gale warning at one o'clock. High water came in mid-afternoon. The seas were breaking over the upper sgeir and flooding up Dune Rock, streaming through the passage between them. I saw a pup caught and swept struggling away from the boulder beach. The little head appeared in the surf, disappeared under the full weight of off-shore breakers. The mother was after it, found it, lost it; she swam to and fro in desperate speed, head and shoulders high out of the water, and often in the wrong direction. The pup was swept to and fro on either side of the lower sgeir; first one and then the other was crashed against the rock. Sometimes the two heads showed together but as often were submerged in the welter of breakers and surf. She kept grabbing at him with her mouth but could never get a hold. In the end a really big sea, a number seven, swept him ashore, high up at my end of the boulder beach. He struggled clear before the next wave and the cow was after him, urging him higher and higher. But he was safe and apparently undamaged except for a blooded face. There was more muzzle sniffing than I'd yet seen.

The wind had veered a little and the glass was rising perceptibly. I tried to pretend that the gale might just be easing, but it wasn't. Another seam was opening at the back of the tent. A one-sided attack with the curved sacking needle would have done more harm than good, and any attempt at walking sewing was obviously impossible. Oh well, must do something: I went down to the tree stranded among the boulders at the head of the beach and sawed off a ten foot length for the earth house. But then I couldn't shift it. I started chopping off the root buttresses to let it roll. Fortunately I had ground and sharpened the little axe and secured the shaft at home. It was only a two-pounder but sharp as a razor and the chips flew most rewardingly. But still the baulk would not move.

I became much involved with this tree. To start with it was fully thirty feet long, broken off at one end and with worn-down roots remaining at the other. It was a beautiful piece of timber, sound and hard and heavy, the annual rings close and even. I thought it was pitch pine. The bark was long gone except for fragments among the roots and the straight trunk was worn smooth and bleached. It must have crossed the Atlantic, and I wondered what cataclysm had sent it on its way, and from where: some turbid Canadian torrent of thaw water perhaps, undermining the river bank until the tree toppled and fell and was swept downstream. I took home a few big chips when I left the island and sent one to the Forest Products Research Laboratory at Princes Risborough, Buckinghamshire.

The tree was a species of larch but it was not possible to say which one. The uniformly narrow growth rings indicated that the tree had probably grown near the Arctic Circle. If it had crossed the Atlantic it was almost certainly tamarack or eastern larch, which grows near the coast as far north as Labrador. But larch of this character is found in North Russia and Siberia, in which case it could be either European or Siberian larch. The timber had been burrowed by longhorn beetle; a well-preserved grub or adult beetle would enable the origin of the tree to be determined more definitely.

I meant to follow up this inviting new world on future cruises in the *Heather*, to look out for more stranded trees on remote beaches and bring back samples for examination. Somehow or other it never got done; perhaps someone else will try.

I noticed that a bit was coming loose at the butt end of my ten foot baulk. I worked away with stone wedges, hammered in with a boulder, and chopped and chopped, and in the end managed to prize off a hefty splinter. I dragged it back to the earth house and dropped it. The prospect looked even more hopeless. Oh well: I took the spade and went back to the beach and started to dig a hole.

I chose the best looking place above the boulder line where the sand cliff was two feet high and faced a scoop. Two lines of stones led towards the dunes as if part of some ancient bothy. The wind came off the grassy dunes so I was not much bothered with blown sand, and I flung the spoil away downwind. The moist sand dug beautifully. The seals would have to put up with a neighbour for a few weeks; anyway they were here every year and I was not. But what I was doing, I reflected, was just what would not be allowed in the future. Then perhaps a boatman with a little badge would bring out a party, no landing allowed, just peer through binoculars. The event was very different: conservancy men roaring up in a rubber dinghy with a big outboard motor, men with rifles and permits coming to shoot the over-numerous pups . . .

In fact I was pleased to see the seals not minding me, working their way inland on either hand. The pups were ranged along the beach-head boulders; the surf licked one or two of them but none was washed away and the tide was ebbing.

Now and then I turned to watch the great combers tower and crash on the beach behind me. I dug for a couple of hours, and crouched in my pit to let the rain squalls go over. As soon as I'd made some depth there was no gale, but I did wonder whether the top of a big spring tide might not sluice in. The clean sand turned to brown with black streaks; I got down to at least a partial stone floor. There had been some sort of construction here, maybe some rough shelter excavated by long gone kelp burners, even the site of an illicit still. Anyway the boulder floor was deep enough; when I stood up the crest of the dunes was just above my head. The only relic was a dark brown seal's tooth.

I went home to feed the puppy and sat in a coma for an hour with him asleep in my lap. After dark I wriggled out again but met the same assault of wind; from indoors the fearfull squalls of rain and booming wind went on unabated. I went exhausted to bed.

Next morning, back into cold wet clothes but with the wind eased to strong, I was cheered by the sight of a gull rising from an afterbirth at the top of the mudslide. The newborn pup lay on the dune top beyond. Here at last was a certain start for a growth series; I marked the pup with a dab of red paint, pushed in a measured stick alongside, and took its first photograph. He was Red One, a male pup born with his muzzle already black. Red Two followed next day; another male pup but white-faced and found when his coat was still matted and wet. They both moved fifty yards during their first day.

The character of the beach had changed in the storm. Rock skeletons had uncovered and sand was heaped in new places; the beach took a fortnight to get back to normal. But my pit in the dunes was neither waterlogged nor fallen in. Showers of hail and snowstorms of suds swept across the Lowlands; the muzzles of sleeping pups flinched when the hailstones struck. After a necessary session of walking sewing I went on a survey of storm casualties and losses. By now I was getting to know individual animals in their customary places, and some had names. This morning some of the cows and pups showed new wounds – raw cuts and bloodied faces. Of the five pups already born on the boulder beach when I landed two were now particular. One, the survivor of his adventure in the storm, became 'Rescued'. The other, 'Scarface', had suffered a bad gash across his muzzle and part of his upper lip hung loose I knew them both for the next month, through weaning and moult to bluecoat, until they were ready to go to sea, or gone. I came to know well the fat weaned pup who lay near my pit in the dunes. It is strange how seal pups, even when crowded, remain loners; they take no notice of each other, the idea of play is non-existent. But this fat pup did try; he tried to play with a waving grass stem, mouthing it, pretending as it blew that it attacked him. It was a poor toy; mostly he slept or wiped his face; he rolled on his back and waved stubby arms, and yawned; he forgot me. Sometimes he woke and gave me a token snarl, but it died down as if he, like me, had got bored with it. Sometimes his wide black eyes watched with mild interest the inexplicable sight of a man shovelling sand.

The sand got tackier as I dug, and then a dribble of water appeared. I dug a small test hole in one corner and it filled to the brim. All the same I took the floor area down to boulders, to finished size and depth.

The day after the storm also marked the beginning of an inland movement of newly arrived seals. 'Severe south-westerly gales' said next evening's forecast. I had come in to get away from wind and chill when I suddenly realized that the breeze had fallen light – an ominous calm, but a delight. I opened up the tent, though the light was going. The Primus burnt unscreened; I made some unsuccessful bread in the tin oven on top. Even a candle was possible. But only for one short evening.

The gales of wind and rain were wearisomely renewed and there were more days of 'nothing much'. When laced-up in the tent how well I knew the sight of wind-streamed moor grass through a chink in the door! I would be bundled up in sweater and fur-lined jacket, gumboots with socks and stockings, trousers lined with pyjamas. But: 'The world is so full of a number of things . . .' Loss of interest is the only failure.

133

Nothing could stale the appeal of newborn pups. Here was one on the beach, already dry and fluffy, the little body loose in its furry sack; a very wavering head lifts from the sand and all innocence gazes from those great black eyes. What a strange world, and the cold surf swills up the sand!

The mere movements of seals were an entertainment; their humping locomotion, the lazy hunching of a bull on his side to move a yard or two, the endearing sickle moon effect on the beach when all the heads and tails went up, hoping to stay dry as the rising tide swilled round them, the pained looks when wetting was inevitable.

The smooth flat sand and a low viewpoint made the looper caterpillar mode of locomotion into a diagram. In spite of its bulk an animal arching backwards showed daylight underneath, and often both bulls and cows would hold their flippers back out of the way and move purely by 'caterpillaring'. The perfect 'tank tracks' across the sand – a broad band pricked along either side by claw marks – indicated purposeful travel. Early in the season when the bulls were wreathed in blubber the whole body quivered as they rippled along like enormous jellies. Pups gradually developed the art from early ineffectual shuffling; they started by using their forelimbs alternately as if trying to walk. Sometimes one of the oversized mittens got stuck underneath the body and the pup tugged and cried trying to get it out. On their first day only, newborn pups tried to use their hind flippers as land paddles, a momentary harking back to aboriginal days when seals were quadrupeds.

A bull on station wiped his nose with the back of his hand, like a stage navvy; he carefully combed his whiskers – parody of a saloon barman, one foot on the brass rail, stroking the froth from a copious moustache. The flippers are hands, so humanly are they used. Sometimes I held a pup's cold hand without protest; they curled their hind flippers into a ball, as if to keep warm.

'The world is so full . . .' The island wrens, busy and domestic-seeming, lived nearly subterranean lives, creeping under boulders among the shore slaters and whirring a few inches above the ground from one crevice to the next; the stronger the wind, the lower the whirr. I put out food for a friendly one who discovered both tent and earth house, and whizzed between the two. A few turnstones and purple sandpipers picked about among the seaside rocks; a gale kept their heads down and made them very tame.

Under a clear sky the dirty pools shone with that incomparable deep brilliant blue particular to Scotland; when close approach broke the sky's reflection they turned ruby red. In rare sunshine it was enough to sit out in the luminous light, and look and look until chilled to the marrow: the sunlit mottled coats of the seals, the sharp white pups, the boulders as smooth and pale as bleached bone, all standing stereoscopic in the low-angled sideways light. At home in after years a particular few minutes of a late autumn evening would come up now and then, when the last of the sunlight was level and lifted every stem of grass across the fields, and a chill breeze stirred; that was a moment of Shillay.

I was often up the hill. A huge boulder near the summit had an overhang which gave perfect shelter. I would sit there and gaze on the grand spread of sea and land laid out below and never a boat or human movement to be seen. On a clear day visibility carried through the Sound and right across to the far side of the Minch where Skye filled the horizon. Sometimes the entrance to the main channel through the Sound was marked by the tiny white scar of Colla Sgeir breaking in a grey sea, with the iron legs of Red Rock and Sgeir Volinish beacons beyond, diminished to a pair of microscopic insects. From sea level Pabbay was a wall across the Sound of Shillay; from up here it resumed an island shape. I could match the map with the real map laid out below, right through to steep Dun-aarin, marking the entrance to the Sound from the Minch. Beyond the western edge of Pabbay stood the rock of Spuir, in the middle of the entrance to the sound between Pabbay and Berneray. Spuir was supposed to harbour cormorants and to grow a crop of wild oats; it remained an unknown.

The view was never uniform; Minch, Sound, Atlantic were

different seas and the sky that roofed them, raining, lowering, holed by sunlight, made an ever-changing patchwork of colour on sea and land. Sometimes I watched all the clobber of heavyweight cloud being pushed away by a freshening breeze and the sun patches coming nearer and nearer on the western ocean. Out in the Atlantic lay the distant arc of final islands, Gasker, even the faraway Flannan Isles, St Kilda, the rocks of Haskeir; I had set foot on all of them. Now I looked out from the summit of Shillay and felt that this island was where I now belonged. This was my place for the time being, whether welcome or not to the proper inhabitants down below.

Upland Shillay is the last outlier of the thin-soiled, free-draining island type, like both Pabbay and Berneray, and Eriskay and Barra down south, where water goes short in summertime and peat is liable to be ferried in, and where alpine plants come down to sea level. Only lowland Shillay is wet. The uplands rise and fall in acre after acre of rolling downs clothed with a close and ancient turf of whitened bent and ling and bright green crowberry, springy to walk on. This poor stuff was goose ground.

One day at the summit two little brown and white birds were hopping about among the rocks and wind-streamed bents, twittering in a pleasant finch-like way: snow buntings, no less. One after the other flung up into the air and was whisked away downwind. Years later, on the Norfolk coast with a grey sea rolling in, a flock of snow buntings threw up into the wind, and I was back on Shillay.

The barnacle geese arrived! The flocks passed to and fro, talking hard, hanging in the wind on motionless wings. They looked at our hilltop and at Little Shillay several times over, but they would not alight. A few days later and they were ranged in a frieze along the skyline of Little Shillay like so many puffins. When I went up the hill with Shilly, we came round rock corners and flushed them like coveys of partridges. The short turf was thick with droppings, the sky was full of parties and companies of geese, and their thrilling talk came down continuously.

Shilly needed a fortnight of tent life before he began to come for walks, fifty-yard outings for a start, but he soon got more adventurous. I used to take him up the hill on a lead or carrying, while the wind blew his ears inside out. Then I let him go and ran downhill full pelt calling him, and he'd follow tumbling and somersaulting. When I took him down to the head of the beach for the first time he was chary of the loose sand, doubtful whether it was safe to walk on. Then he found it was splendid stuff, he dashed about in it, he dug and romped and tried to eat it. I introduced him to one of the mudslide pups. They sniffed momentarily muzzle to muzzle but neither showed the least interest – two young carnivores each wildly outside the other's experience. In a few days time it was different, when Shilly found a moulting pup too fat to move. He soon discovered that its snapping reach was limited, and he dashed and he barked and dragged himself full length on his tummy and played all the puppy tricks and had a great time. Poor seal pup – it could only open its mouth and vent the stock reaction of a husky snarl. Tears of helpless frustration rolled from its eyes, it beat its silly flipper, so *useless*, it turned its head away in despair. Shilly never learnt the trick of moving a pup by tweaking its hindquarters, as the bulls and cows did when they wanted one out of the way. He learnt to be more careful after a livelier pup 'got him one' – he just lay and whimpered. He was soon making his own expeditions from the tent and finding unwilling playmates for himself; I heard the yapping from afar. Not many puppies can have gone through the dung-eating stage on the droppings of wild geese and the pasty excreta of baby seals.

My sand pit in the dunes gradually developed into Dune House. A fat pup took to lying in it and when I hustled him out with the spade he expelled a trail of evil-smelling dung. Seals are coarse! They sneeze and spray out gobs of phlegm at one end and fart freely at the other. They are full of roundworms and are covered with wounds and sores. They can't groom themselves so they wipe their faces and scratch the rest. The bulls gave off a powerful reek and even the pups soon develop the beginnings of it. They all love wallowing in stinking black mud.

The pit was something of a seal trap. I happened to catch sight of one of my pups, Red One, go sniffing over the edge; he overbalanced and disappeared in a flurry of flippers. I cut ramps on either side to make easy routes between beach and dunes. A seal on the roof would be disastrous.

Seepage water soon submerged the floor. It would. I shovelled back sand to cover it up and the sand, being obliging stuff, mopped it up and made a more or less dry floor, with the loss of only six inches of headroom. The walls began to slump and collapse, in spite of the network of sea couch roots through the sand. I should have to line the whole thing with beach boulders and that would leave only a tiny den.

The famous castaway tree yielded all the roofing timber. A big baulk made the lintel for the doorway, rolled and levered into place; another length made the main fore and aft beam, and six big splinters provided subsidiary rafters. The final butt end I inched into place in front of the doorway as a seal barrier. The wet stones lining the walls made a pretty pattern of all the monochromes between white and black, and all the colours of reds and pinks and yellows and browns and grey-greens. It was done, a bit at a time, in ten days from start to finish. While I was finishing off the job, on a day of blowing drizzle, a splendid flight of fifteen wild swans beat past along the line of coast, low down, talking together, making slow headway against the wind. They appeared from the mist and disappeared into it. I set up a camera to record 'before and after' the final roofing with the rickcloth. It was dim inside but lighter than the tent, and wonderfully quiet and still. It would have made an adequate refuge but it was never called on. I merely used it as a handy and sheltered observation point; no seal ventured on the roof and the tide never reached the doorway.

I thought myself a herdsman attending his sea cattle but if anyone was obviously not wanted, it was me. A mating couple inadvertently surprised in a pool broke off their connection and splashed away; a cow left her suckling pup and jerked snarling towards me, pup left mouth in mid-air; even the pups snarled their stock reaction. But it was I who was anxious for pups being washed to and fro in the surf, while their mothers took no notice. My good will was void after centuries of clubbing.

Dislocation of a seal colony is only averted by keeping still in one place. Of course I found some tolerant, if not tame, bulls and cows and I used to spend half a day at a time with them: the best compliment I was paid was when one of the bulls I was sitting with, turned his back on me, and slept. But the seals were much wilder than last time, though I behaved just as carefully. Possibly, the first time, my coming in mid-season had made a difference, when the seals were already committed to the island, whereas this time I had come in near the beginning. I left them strictly alone early and late so that at least they had some sixteen hours in every twenty-four without disturbance. Judging by the sounds night activity was similar to daytime except that the cows were more prone to their wailing songs. When I shone a strong torch on to the mudslide the glittering eyes of pups and adults were reflected back. The early morning sounds carrying on the breeze into the tent compared with a farmer's bedroom; he'd know what was going on in the stockyard outside, and so did I.

All the same there remained something odd and unexplained about this particular season. It was the same year that Seton Gordon called at Gasker in a fishery cruiser and on 6 November found 'upwards of 100 pups lying dead' out of a total of 700-800. On Shillay an end of October count of live pups of all ages was less than half that of three years before, though nearly a fortnight later in the season – 76 as against 192.

What I thought I was doing was modest enough but the results were even more modest. No serious zoological studies evidently, no branding or tagging of pups, no daily weighings, no 'lactation trials' or the like of that. Natural curiosity is one thing; the compulsion to put one's name to a learned paper, however minor, is quite another. There are other ways

139

of coming to terms with wild animals; there is no place for wonder in the *Proceedings of the Royal Zoological Society*. I wished to spend some time with a chosen few of them in a particular place. My case was puzzling to local gossip in Harris; he wasn't from a University or from the Government, he had no grant or official backing; perhaps he was taking photographs for a newspaper? I feel sympathy for students wanting to go to some wild corner of the globe and trying to think up some acceptable excuse, some trumped-up research project, for getting a grant. Good grounds for an expedition to Spitzbergen would be to look at the view. Let some fragment of the earth remain unmapped.

Hours of watching from the tent doorway! A gull with a blood-red head was perched on an injured pup, pecking holes in its back. The pup was still alive. Nature is all very well but there are limits. I had brought a .22 pistol with me, in case of I don't know what, so now I got it out and went down to the beach and put a bullet through the pup's head. It was the only time I fired the gun.

A heavily gravid cow lay on the beach, moving uneasily, heaving and panting with open mouth; her time must be imminent. The local bull approached, they sniffed muzzle to muzzle. She gave birth – the gory heap was suddenly there. She writhed away to break the connection, turned to sniff the pup. A lick of surf reached it, turned it round. The cow lay below it, broadside on to the sea. The little red heap remained inert. She couldn't keep still, kept shifting about, sniffing at it. The tide was ebbing. She left it and approached the bull, waved her head at him – he gave ground. She went on and climbed right on top of the upper sgeir – the first time I had seen a seal there – and stopped and peered this way and that. She slithered down again and went back to the motionless pup. She stayed with it for an hour. A gull sidled up; she lifted her head, threatening; the gull gave way, but came back; she lunged and snapped at it, the gull floated off. She snapped at another gull flying close over. But they had the pup before long.

Seal births are seldom witnessed: suckling, mating, fighting, courtship, bickering – it all goes on openly – but seldom a birth is seen. Probably it usually happens under cover of darkness. The single birth I saw in full was that of this still-born pup.

The actual place of birth varies from colony to colony. (I stick to the old-fashioned word 'colony' and leave the silly-sounding term 'rookery' to the penguins and Antarctica.) The place of birth is the cow's choice and it is an index of the extent of her committment to land; the territorial behaviour of bulls and the self-imposed swimming lessons of the pups stem from it. Shillay is a halfway house. Far to the north, on Rona, some cows give birth hundreds of yards inland and uphill and they certainly remain there, fasting, throughout their pups' suckling; mating then takes place with the local bull on bare ground. Far to the south, on the narrow stony beaches of Wales, the cows are always in close touch with the sea. The bulls hardly ever come ashore and mating takes place in open water. The pups are pushed by the tide to the foot of the cliffs and are forced into early swimming, or drowning. On Shillay, mating was in pools and wallows and in the surf or afloat, and sometimes on the sand or turf. Some of the cows remained inland – one was nearly three hundred yards from the beach – but many kept in touch with the sea. Sometimes I saw a cow pause in the surf and drink thirstily before launching herself.

This graduation of breeding behaviour appears to be forced on the animals by topography, rather than indicating any progressive emancipation from the land. Seals are both con-servative and adaptable: conservative in their obstinate return to traditional grounds even when overcrowded or harassed by man, but adabtable in the variety of sites they can turn to use, from Baltic ice to steep rocks, to island grass and shores, to pinched-in stony beaches and dim sea caves.

Shillay is unique in having the only proper shell sand beach in all Scotland where seals haul out to breed. It made for easy landing but there was one penalty against which they were defenceless, and that was blowing sand. They hated it but could not escape. In a dry gale rheumy-eyed bulls and cows and pups were all the same – their eyes encrusted with sand and streaming with tears. A sleeping pup lay half buried in drifting sand; he woke with his eyes full of sand, he kept wiping his face and whiskers, and tried in vain to turn away from the sandblast. I had so often envied the seals their indifference to storm and cold and wet; now for once they were unhappily at a loss and only I could get away.

I was the first to camp on Shillay but in later years professional zoologists followed me. Dr Morton Boyd stayed with his wife and a friend for ten days, Professor H. R. Hewer and party came twice, all of them more acute observers than myself and with the advantage of experience of grey seal breeding grounds elsewhere.

It was Morton Boyd who noted that the crowd of seals on the beach early in the season comprised about equal numbers of bulls and cows. (The middle of the beach, as mentioned earlier, is neutral ground and the close pack of seals there is a special feature of Shillay.) Hewer saw the same thing; the bulls looked youngish but the cows were all near their term and repelled attempts at molestation. I noticed how the mid-beach crowd diminished as the season went on; from mid-October onwards the space was sometimes nearly empty.

Bulls holding territory mate only with cows within their territory, and virgin cows are never seen in a breeding colony. So how does a virgin cow first get mated, and where? These young non-territorial bulls were available for any cow that would have them, but where were the virgins?

Other seal islands have offlying sgeirs and skerries where masses of seals are seen to congregate at the beginning of the breeding season. It is reasoned – speculated – in the absence of direct observation, that this must be where the first impregnations occur. But Shillay has no offlying skerries and I never saw any seals on the nearest available hauling out place, the admittedly rather unsuitable south-east corner of Little Shillay. Could the answer be, in the water?

Professor Hewer also noted what he at first called the 'victory roll' of bulls on Shillay. I saw it commonly after a confrontation with another bull and thought it an engaging quirk

142

of locomotion – the animal rolled right over and completed a revolution, sometimes twice over; it looked lazy. But later on Hewer realized that this manoeuvre marked the edge of a bull's territory; it wasn't so much a victory roll as the declaration of a boundary. The cows too roll on one side and flap the upper flipper and hoo-hoo at an interested bull, and then complete the roll. That was their declaration of their own and their pup's ground.

The interesting thing about the bulls' roll was that it was largely confined to Shillay. A roll requires reasonably flat ground but even in colonies where the terrain is suitable for rolling, it has rarely been seen. Is this then a phenomenon peculiar to the seals of Shillay and thus a piece of evidence that breeding colonies are discrete and self-contained? Or is there a free come and go amongst them?

Some play has been made with the variable coat colour of bulls, the suggestion being that different seal islands display a differing dominant colour, and thus support the argument that each island harbours a self-contained population. I found this something of a false trail. A good light and a dry coat are required for a start, which is not exactly commonplace. Try deciding the exact colour of a sea-wet pelt, let alone those stained with peat mud or plastered with sand. Dry coats have a thick pile like a carpet, quite different from the sleek plastered appearance of a pelt newly out of the sea. A seal lying half-submerged in a pool, with a stripe of dry fur along its back, appears to have a mane. A dry coat seen against the light looks silvery and almost fluffy.

I spent, or wasted, a lot of time on coat colour. Bulls look brindled when the darker blotches are separate and a lighter colour shows between; the coat looks uniform when the dark patches run together. 'Grey seal' is an odd name. The colour of bulls ranges from various browns to greys and blacks, and although the cows are commonly some sort of grey, some are as brown as bulls. A rather moth-eaten brown was perhaps the commonest colour for Shillay bulls but the browns varied much in tone and included a rich chestnut. Greys were generally a mottled iron grey and an occasional very handsome

143

beast was uniformly mole coloured. Old bulls had much paler heads, some almost silvery white, giving a suitable impression of senior citizens. There were cows of various browns among the general more or less greys and their undersides ranged from cream to buff to a tawny yellow, but always marked with darker spots. One particularly beautiful cow I called Leopard, which was a fair description. My unhelpful conclusion in the matter of coat colour was 'a mixed old lot'.

It was, incidentally, a richly brown coated cow who demonstrated how all the pools and puddles and wallows of the seal ground must have originated. She was an unusually stalwart mother who would not leave her pup but her fierceness towards me brought out symptoms of acute unhappiness: she jerked towards me, open-mouthed and snarling and howling, but her eyes streamed with tears, and rolled and showed the whites. To start with she lay in tall brown moor grass at the foot of the hill, very much looking the part of wild animal in its lair, though one that had unaccountably lost its limbs. The grass was soon flattened and matted. By wriggling and rolling and scratching first with one claw and then the other, she had soon worked herself a scoop. She ended up by lying nearly submerged in a home-made bath.

Whether or not the various and varied islands are self-contained, it seems most likely that once an animal, bull or cow, has spent a season in a particular colony it will return there for the rest of its life. It seems likely that most pups will eventually return to the island of their birth, and it also seems likely that new grounds are colonised by younger rather than older cows.

With hindsight I came to think of Shillay as just about an ideal island from the seals' point of view, given only freedom from human interference. The landing was as easy as any in Scotland and better than most; only a few pups were washed away and drowned. There was plenty of room inland, plenty of inviting pools and wallows and, for one reason or another, the animals kept themselves relatively thin on the ground while remaining sufficiently gregarious. The elements of quarrelling – bulls challenging or repelling each other, cows

144

The pup called St. Kilda, in the pool where he learnt to swim

The tents with boulder beach and main beach beyond

Main beach, Shillay – neutral ground

Shilly with an unwilling playmate

The sad bull 'Greyman'

The dune house re-visited by the author

defending pups, cows repelling bulls, cows in search of
strayed pups, pups in search of mothers – all this leads to
wastefulness and dead pups unless there is enough room. On
overcrowded grounds suckling is perpetually interrupted; on
Shillay the pups usually suckled peacefully until full-fed while
their mothers lay with closed eyes. Instead of overcrowding
the island, some cows (though of unknown origin) went and
founded a new colony on nearby Coppay. The more crowded
the place, it seems, the more cows to each bull and certainly
the greater the mortality of pups. Peace and success depend
on living room. Shillay appeared to strike a happy medium
and perhaps that was reflected in the overall impression of
slumber.

# III

I usually attended the weather forecasts three times a day, the
preoccupation was as bad as that. One midday I picked up a
hint and so was careful not to miss the six o'clock. It was
coming at last! – 'a rapidly intensifying anti-cyclone off
north-west Scotland', and tomorrow was to have 'sunny
periods', those were the exact words. The evening was overcast and threatening but the breeze fell light. I cooked up a
tinful of candle ends and poured it smoking hot down the
worst of the cobbled tent seams. After dark I had the door
open. The sky cleared to stars and a half moon, the wet sand
glittered like silver, the seals' songs carried on the quiet air,
the sound of the sea was reduced to the break of harmless little
waves on the beach.

Next morning I flung open both the double door flaps for
the first time and left them loose. The tent stood slack with its
ribs showing. For the first time I shook out my nasty bedding
and hung it out to air; the cloud of feathers drifted gently
away. It was enough just to be about, to do nothing. A holiday, a saint's day!

This beatitude is entirely Hebridean and must mostly come
from sheer contrast with the norm. Everywhere are the signs
of scouring wind and rain, the bare hills and rocks and sea,

145

but suddenly there is no wind. Yet it has a magic in its own right. The nearest English equivalent for this island morning would have been an early, pearly, overcast, cool fresh dawn in June.

I was going up the hill to see whether St Kilda might be in sight when I spied a dot on the sea far back in the Sound. A look through glasses showed a white boat with two men standing aft, bobbing on the swell and heading my way. It was Murdo right enough! At this moment a shaft of sunlight struck through; the geese uprose from the hill, the air was full of their cackling as the big birds circled black and white in the sunshine above. I went back and hastily cleaned myself up, scraped off the stubble, dragged a comb through matted hair and scrubbed my yellowed teeth. The boat anchored off and Murdo and his mate came ashore in a hefty small boat, too heavy to pull up. Shilly and I met them on the beach. Murdo was expecting me to come off, so, no provisions, no rum, no cigarettes, yet he had brought the mail. I showed them round my works. Murdo looked at the abandoned walls of the earth house and said, 'Well anyway, it'll still be there when we've all gone'.

Give me another fortnight, I asked him, and then come and get me on the first fit day. The boat backed off and was gone with a whiff of paraffin smoke. I went back up the hill and the seals came ashore again. The sun was actually hot. The dried grass was crisp to walk on. My boots were powdered white with crystallized salt.

I sensed that this day, 20 October, was going to be a turning point and so it turned out. There were only two more gales during the rest of the month and October rainfall (at Kyles) fell just short of ten inches. Twice more I aired my bedding. On one halcyon day I went about in shirtsleeves. Looking back, the beginnings now seemed quite old-fashioned: securing and furnishing the tent, digging the ditches, housetraining Shilly, enduring all those awful gales.

I went my rounds with new heart. The season was moving on. By now the first crop of pups were smooth and chubby bluecoats, wandering, playing in the pools or already gone to sea. The heaps of shed hair scattered about looked as if a number of sheep had died. Brand new bulls kept arriving, in hopes of replacing the spent. The Lowlands were now well occupied, with cows and bulls and pups lying on the landward side of both ponds, and scattered among the boulders and pools of the peninsula.

Furthest inland of all was the pup I called St Kilda from his having been born by a pool not far short of the western cliffs and thus nearest of all to that speck in the western ocean. Throughout his fortnight's suckling he lay out on the cliff-edge grass with his mother either nearby or in the pool below. Then one day as he was weaning he joined his mother in the pool. During the next fortnight he learnt to swim and dive, but just to be in the water was enough; it was his element now and he loved it – to lie and float loose in it, to roll lazily with forepaws held to sides and head thrown back, so that all that showed was the turn of a pale belly. And he, like the rest, enjoyed the beginnings of power, giving a hard twisting thrust and going under with a swirl. He cruised with his head awash, blowing bubbles. He was a cheerful wight, one of Shilly's friends and less unwilling than the rest. He would get a grip on the bank with his hands and crane high to see over the edge. When Shilly approached for a muzzle sniff he took fright and dived explosively but he was soon up again and ready for another look over the bank.

My best and longest lasting friend among the pups was Blackman. He was one of the original boulder beach pups, newly born when I landed. He became particularized and called Rescued after his near shave in the storm of 7 October but soon became better known as Blackman. He would let me hold his hand and stroke his beautiful new coat with no more than a plaintive look from his liquid eyes and a murmur of protest.

The end of babyhood was a happy time of life for the pups. Full-fed and moulted, neither hungry nor itching with half-shed hair, without the cares of getting a living and innocent of wariness, they wandered from pool to pool, splashing and playing by themselves. It was as charming a stage as any, the

147

sleek domed heads, sometimes rising encumbered with water weeds, the forward looking wide black eyes that gave them a hint of humanity. They seemed to be in finishing school, or even on holiday, before hunger or some inward clock should drive them to sea.

Here on Shillay they could learn elementary swimming in inland pools instead of in the rough sea. Two such learners appeared in my water supply pool and churned it into smelly mud. But in spite of their practice the first pups to appear at sea still looked amateurish, flourishing their hind flippers ineffectually and not yet able to dive properly. Pups at this stage appeared to be too buoyant to remain submerged; they slept or rested in their pools with an inch or two of back showing above the surface. One pup lay in a pool so small that he only just had room to turn. I took a stopwatch to him and timed half a dozen submersions; the shortest was three quarters of a minute, the longest nearly four minutes, with only a few seconds of noisy breathing between whiles.

I also took my portable wireless to both pups and cows. Seals are supposed to be fond of music. An orchestral concert was going on so I took the set to the upper pond where a group of cows were lying, and played it across the water. There was a good deal of raising of heads and craning of necks in mild enquiry but of course the sound was not nearly loud enough; what was wanted was bagpipes through a loud hailer. I tried it on a moulted pup at close range but he did not like it at all and floundered into the nearest pool.

At last I was being treated with some show of indifference as long as I was very careful but occasionally a bull behaved so out of character and seemed to be so completely self-absorbed that I doubted whether even a man with a club would have registered much impression. It was a cow's birth blood which brought about this total concentration. One morning a cow lay with her newborn pup at the top of the mudslide and all around the grass was stained red. She left the pup and a newcomer bull came panting urgently uphill. I was nearby but he came on regardless, of me or of his own bulk or of the steep slope, and he found the blood and snuffled all over it. He seemed to be simply unaware of my existence. At other times I saw bulls roll and squirm on their backs in birth blood, like a dog rolling in offal, or they would twitch a young pup out of the way and then squirm on the place where it had been lying. Just as the cows recognized their pups only by smell, by muzzle to muzzle sniffing, I wondered whether the bulls were marking the ground by laying their own smell or whether they were just anticipating ownership of the cow.

I did not discover just how long it was after giving birth until a cow was ready for connection. Certainly mating took place during lactation. I saw a pup fed and then its mother yield to the bull a couple of yards away. I saw a bull and cow indulge in protracted snapping and snarling and then the bull so far mistake his sparring partner as to try to mount her. A first class vicious fight followed: the bull grabbed at her and got her nose by mistake; blood and sand and water went flying. She got away breathing fast and dripping blood, she wiped her face and smeared blood all over herself. The pup she went back to was barely a week old.

All the hoo-hooing of cow to bull, and snapping and flipper flapping, was it repulsion or invitation? Probably, being female and oestrus coming on, it was a bit of both: stages of courtship. Certainly the bulls seemed ready to try it on at any time and would take an unwilling cow by the scruff of her neck, but such rough advances were seldom, I think, fulfilled.

In the end came resolution. Two were willing and two were joined and lay afloat or ashore or aground for an absorbed, comfortable-looking and not unduly thrustful half hour. The cow lies supine but sometimes hoo-howls and waves her free flipper and twists her head to make mock bites. The bull embraces with a flipper and sometimes bites on to the scruff of her neck. His organ is very large and bright red and has a sort of frilly knob on the end which looks exactly like a sea anemone and which presumably helps retention. The red shaft shows between the cow's rear flippers.

On the two or three occasions I disturbed a couple it was

purely by mistake; the bull had to hump away over the rocks with that tender piece extruded. But apologetics were hardly called for. I saw a cow finish suckling and go straight to a nearby bull and start advances. They scrapped, he tried to mount and it was another case of his grabbing her nose by mistake. She was streaming blood and he was erect, thrusting into the sand and against her sand-plastered back, trying to get in. Then he had to break off to go through a show of fangs and snarling against the next door bull.

Serious and bloody bull fights were unusual. The common pattern was challenge by one bull and withdrawal by the other but if after confrontation and a show of teeth neither would give way then battle was inevitable. One I watched in the surf lasted about twenty minutes. It looked like a wrestling match at first: one shoved hard against the other's neck and tried to bite, while keeping his own neck and shoulder under adversary's neck to prevent him biting. Thus deadlock. They broke away and catch as catch can followed, each snatching and snapping, both bleeding and both seeming to get dreadful holds on the other's hide. The battle was waged without pause, to and fro in the sandy surf, so that sometimes only a threshing and splashing was to be seen, and momentarily upflung flippers and tails. They parted only to come at each other again and each in turn got damaging-looking holds on the other's rear flippers. The end of it was a draw. They appeared to part in mutual exhaustion; both hauled out a yard or two up the beach and lay flat out, panting with open mouths.

After their weeks of vigilance and starvation, fights and expense of seed, bulls are even more spent than the wasp-waisted dry cows and have to face oncoming winter in very poor shape. The cows' annual shoregoing is much shorter, only about three weeks, for they have finished mating and are back at sea again within a few days of weaning their pups. And only the best of the pups are in good case; no weaner with a figure less than barrel-shaped has much hope of survival, for independence to a pup means moulting and fasting and then learning to fend for itself entirely without instruction in wild seas at the beginning of winter.

By chance the two pups I was following through from birth to independence, Red One and Red Two, turned out to be one of each in their prospects of survival. Red One would be all right; his good mother suckled him regularly for a full fortnight and his moult was as good as over within a week of weaning. He started pool bathing on his twentieth day. After that I met him from time to time travelling among the ponds and pools. Red Two also had a fortnight's suckling but it must have been intermittent; he put on some weight and bulk, but not enough, and he remained poorly and backward. Once I saw him trying to suck a full grown pup. He had little hope of a future. Always the best looking pups were those whose mothers lay near them all the time. But the pups would wander and the cows could be so silly.

A cow offers her teats in the surf, the pup tries to suck but the next wave washes him off. She is after him like a terrier chasing a ball but is ineffectual when she does catch him. At sea or ashore cows could only move their pups by leading them. And the routine of recognition caused trouble: a small pup on the beach was approached by a very large cow whom I took to be its mother; she held it down with a flipper the better to sniff and ended by actually rolling on it, but it was not hers after all and when rightful mother did arrive there was a fight right on top of the pup.

Any wandering pup, crying and searching, was as much a trouble maker as any adult; disturbed cows snarled and wailed in discomfort, split between leaving their own pups and driving away the stranger. But if a pup persisted with the wrong cow he was in for some vicious biting and shaking. I saw a cow give way to the tension and so snap at a stranger, and dig so fast with a flipper that divots of turf went flying; and the pup retreated with a patch of blood on either side of his head. No wonder that some of them failed to make the grade.

The Orphan was a sad case. I knew when and where he was born, at the edge of the dunes by the so-called bothy, but I never saw his mother. He was easily identified by an unusual

151

brown tinge to his puppy coat. On his third day and still apparently unfed he appeared at the top of the mudslide, having climbed aimlessly over the dunes. He made his way down to the boulder beach, to a pocket of sand against the lower sgeir. He lay there all day until the tide pushed him up. In the evening I carried him back to his birthplace. He hadn't much struggle left; his little limbs were stone cold and wet, but there was still some warmth in his armpits and his heart was going well. Next morning a newborn pup (Sunday's Child) and its mother lay on the same pocket of sand and close by there was the Orphan back again. He shuffled to the cow; she rebuffed him but he kept nosing her flank. She didn't know what to do, with her own pup on one side and a stranger on the other. She opened her mouth at the Orphan, waved a flipper and shifted uncomfortably. He kept trying. She turned on him and in a clumsy but gentle way smothered him with a flipper. This time he did withdraw, but soon came back. Her own pup, lying at the back of her head and not yet fed, now began to bawl. The circumstance of her own pup crying and a nuzzling stranger seemed to strike an uneasy balance. She no longer rebuffed the stranger and even lay with her head down. I could see her soft belly give as the Orphan dug at her with his muzzle. He certainly got hold of a teat and I think got a feed because afterwards he withdrew of his own accord, and lay on his back with his paws across his chest and slept, his belly pink with the cow's birth blood. She tried her own pup, snuffed and pawed him, rolled over for him, but although he was crying he wouldn't search for the teats, he merely shuffled round her head. She gave up and humped away on to the boulders; both pups slept.

When her own pup woke and bawled, she tried again and lay this way and that but it was still no good. In the afternoon it was the same again. She shuffled about but ended with her own pup at the back of her head while the Orphan stole what looked like a satisfactory feed. At last but still on his first day her pup did find the place and sucked for twenty minutes. He had another feed in the evening. From then on Sunday's

Child flourished and was doing very well when I left the island ten days later.

The morning after his stolen feeds the Orphan was trailing yellow dung, but he was a poor wizened little thing, hunched up, dirtied with his own dung, one eye bunged up with sand. During the following days he must have managed to steal an occasional feed because his rear end was smeared with fresh dung. He began to moult prematurely on his tenth day when he was no bigger than Sunday's Child at half his age. Next day he lay dead.

Castaway was lucky. He was washed off Mainbeach on his second day and washed up again at the foot of the boulder beach; his mother found him and tried to lead him to safety but he couldn't manage it. She came and offered her teats while he was half awash; the sea soon carried him away again. The little head was bobbing fifty yards out while his mother did no more than keep near him. In the end the sea sent him back and sluiced him into a crevice, where he stuck. His mother waited on a rock above until the tide turned and left him temporarily safe. He cried all the afternoon but was not fed until dusk, when he scrambled down to rocks below high water mark. I expected him to be washed off again, but his adventures turned out to be over. They both stayed thereabouts for the next fortnight until he was weaned and his mother duly kept company with the nearest bull. I was told in Harris that after an October storm pups were occasionally washed up on Scarasta sands, having been carried right round Toe Head; sometimes they were still alive.

A late-comer to the neutral park on the beach was a poorly iron-grey bull who looked gaunt and very old. Day after day he lay there, only moving with the tide, without ambition, taking no part in the life around him. There was something very much the matter with Greyman; his body heaved silently, racked with an inward cough. He kept opening his mouth, as if to get rid of something, as if to be sick; he lay with eyes closed. I supposed that his lungs were full of worms and that he was slowly dying. He gave me the clue to how neutrality was declared. When threatened he gave the cow reaction, he

153

rolled over on his side and vibrated the top flipper and made to snap. Others did the same and thus the neutral area was preserved in spite of jealously guarded bull territories on either side.

I had a favourite lie behind the massive driftwood baulk on the beach (of which one end was my tent table). From there I watched a group of cows generally to be seen near the base of Shelter Skerry, the cows Leopard, Coffee, Wall-eye and Loose-claw. Wall-eye was blind in one eye, Loose-claw had a nail sticking out like a dagger from one flipper.

Here was a game of consequences. A bull was sparring with Loose-claw in the surf. He had a flipper thrown over her and was trying to mount, but she wanted to get back to her pup. She tried to go, he tried to jump her. When she broke away and started up-beach, he followed. He was soon trespassing but he got so far up that next door bull, approaching in haste, took him in the rear – he was cut off. He turned quick enough for the sea but as both were moving fast there was no place for preliminary challenge. They charged into each other at speed for a short sharp battle. Trespasser got back unharmed to his own ground but left Victor with a blooded shoulder. Victor now pursued and caught up with Loose-claw. They sparred, he tried to mount, she broke away. She found her pup among the beach-head boulders, went through the recognition sniffs and in fits and starts led him back to the sea. She started to feed him on dry sand but they ended up in the surf; he suckled intermittently for fully half an hour. She was looking very gaunt by now and the pup remarkably plump; in such cases it almost looked as if pup should be feeding mother.

Suckling appeared to end by mutual consent; the gaunt-hipped cow offered milkless teats, the pup lost interest and went off to moult and that was the end of brief motherhood.

Time and again wonder and freshness struck anew. I got accustomed but never used to solitary residence on the island of Shillay: sitting among those big extraordinary animals by a dirty pond; sweeping the ground with binoculars from up the hill; blue shadows creeping across the white beach in rare late sunlight; my own long shadow ahead on the brown grass when I took a bucket on an early morning walk to the water pool.

Having had a taste of halcyon weather, and knowing it to be possible, I was difficult to please. On a clear night it was galling to know that daylight would have brought a flood of sunshine. But such a night! I went up the hill with Shilly in brilliant moonlight. The lop-sided moon was high over Pabbay, the glittering track across the water joined the two islands. Cotton-wool clouds in a starlit sky and not even a breeze, a still night by the sea; and this was the same wind-worried country of sour and sodden bog and stone, habitually swept by mist and rain. The dirty ponds and pools were silver, the broad uncovered beach dotted with black sack-shapes, the little waves broke one after another and sluiced silently up the sand. It seemed wrong to speak out loud, calling to the dog. I lost any sense of place. Impossible to believe that the overcrowded British Isles still included country like this, as wild as anywhere in the temperate world. But it was not British, nor even Scottish, there was no reason why a boat's crew should speak Gaelic; the island was innominate, boreal – farther and farther away until only the bare bones of beauty were left, rock and sea and sand.

I opened up the tent for the night and lay in bed listening to the little waves and the seals' soprano songs, the baby cries and the passing of geese overhead.

Once I saw an aeroplane. On one wet day the hydro-electric station at Loch Sloy was opened by the Queen, so I heard. On another George Bernard Shaw died, at 4.59 a.m. November came in. I lay in bed listening to the rain with Shilly asleep on my feet until eventually and as usual: 'Well Shilly, time we were getting up.' But early November brought a nice quiet spell. The boat would be coming any day now, today or tomorrow or the next day. I struck and packed the small tent and took the roof off Dune House. I went my rounds and made my farewells, to poor old Greyman with his hacking cough, to Loose-claw and Wall-eye and Coffee and Leopard, to Sunday's Child and Castaway and St Kilda and

155

Midway, to happy Red One and sad Red Two and most of all to my best friend Blackman who was six weeks old now and still not gone to sea but who still let me hold his hand and stroke his velvety coat.

As soon as I saw a white boat coming I started packing and carting stuff down to the beach. I didn't take much notice of the boat until it was near and then I realized it wasn't Murdo the lobsterman's but Mackenzie the grazier's, and full of sheep. The boat anchored off and load after dinghy-load of sheep were ferried inshore and tipped into the water. No one came ashore or took any notice of me. I waded into the surf and shouted to Mackenzie's son in the dinghy. Was Murdo coming? Aye, I think he will be. Could he get a message to him to be certain sure of coming? Aye, I think we could. But they were going somewhere else first. I acquired the irrelevant information that they were landing forty-two wethers. The wethers walked up the beach in single file and preserved their order as they wandered away up the hill and disappeared. The boat went away and diminshed to a white dot. I waited about until it was too late for another boat and then angrily started carting all my goods back to the tent, a 200-yard round trip each time. Shilly was feeling homeless so I started the refurnishing with box and blanket, to which he sensibly retired and slept. I retrieved some unappetising thrown-away food.

I imagined the two white launches back at Leverburgh, both empty and each saying to the other 'I thought for sure . . .' Really I blamed myself, I should have insisted on going with Mackenzie, I ought to have understood by now the meaning of that Hebridean 'I thought for sure.' Well anyway, my belongings had been spared a voyage in sheep dung.

Now the weather would break and that would be that, indefinitely. Back to the blasted weather forecasts, and already the message was 'strong, easterly'. I now realized how badly I wanted to get off but I also felt a queer regret; there should be someone else coming, someone to turn over to, to demonstrate what was going on, and who was who, otherwise it would all be wasted.

The setting sun appeared below a bank of cloud, a true

November's crimson orb. It looked more like mist and a touch of frost than wind. In bed I needed my whole stock of sweaters and bedding and then the blankets were wet with dew.

I woke to a flood of sunshine and a cold north-easterly breeze, and no more than a breeze: perfection. But I wasn't going to do any more hopeful packing and carting. Halfway through the day when I was down on the beach with a camera a white boat suddenly appeared round the corner. This time it was Murdo. He closed the rocks below the tent: 'Are you coming off today?' (Blimey, I should think I bloody well am.) He'd been putting down creels on the other side of Toe Head and had seen a few seal pups on Coppay as he'd passed by on the way to Shillay. The tide was right and loading from the rocks was much easier once the dinghy lines had been rigged. Poor Shilly was at a loss, his home was gone, and when there was nothing left but heaps of boulders and driftwood he lay chewing at one of his toys, an ancient sheep's skull, in lovely, wasted sunshine. He was shy of boat and crew and was soon seasick.

I looked back: Well, the main object of the exercise had been 'to see what like it was' and in that I could hardly have helped succeeding, right enough.

Home-coming was something of an anti-climax. No one saw us arrive and as soon as the heap of goods was piled on the jetty Murdo went off to lift his creels. When I found my hosts they were just going out. I carted everything into the back room where Shilly settled among the gear he knew as well as I did. The longed-for bath water was cold.

But the delight of indoors! I wandered from room to room on a level floor on soft carpets. Silence! Supper, sitting up to a brightly lit table; and when we drove to the post office after dark a little bare aspen sapling at the roadside was illuminated by the headlights. It was a sudden pleasure and so was the rough road and the car itself; and then there was a full-sized bed with cool/warm clean sheets. If only everyday life could be like this! – but you have to bang your head against a brick wall first for the pleasure of stopping.

There was frost at night and unbroken sunshine for two short flawless days. I took Shilly and climbed to the summit of Roneval with camera and clumsy tripod and a last saved-up sheet of colour film. Visibility was fifty miles. I sat up there for an hour looking at the marvellous spread of sea and islands. Down below bits of haymaking was still going on; it had been one of those harvest seasons 'the worst in the memory of old men'. Now peat smoke from the crofts rose in the silent sunshine. Shillay looked very small.

Next day Shilly and I set off on our long drive southwards, towards fresh-turned furrows and big trees standing stationary with coloured leaves.

# *Epilogue*

I kept in touch with Shillay for nine more years after my autumn residence and I went back four times, always curious to see how my monuments were faring. The first time was during the summer following that brilliant day of November sunshine when Shilly had been so disconsolate at the loss of his home, and shy with strange men, and then seasick. It was late July and we chose a bad day. A south-westerly breeze made the bay lumpy and the rocks beyond the boulder beach into a dead lee shore laced with surf; Shelter Skerry was rapidly disappearing as the tide rose towards high water. But I wanted to take Brian, on his first visit, on a personally conducted tour and there was also the matter of storm petrels to be looked into. No less an authority than the naturalist William MacGillivray had reported storm petrels on Shillay in 1830 and Harvie-Brown had found them again in his time. The island had not changed and there was no reason why the generations of petrels should not have continued.

We let go the anchor, went astern to dig it in, and waited to see the boat settled. So did a few interested seals. This time the anchor cable was only rope, which did not inspire confidence. We landed to windward, at the base of Shelter Skerry, hauled up the dinghy, and once again I trod the clean white sand. Dune House was as good as new! The seal ponds were bone dry with lush green banks. The watercourses of winter had dried up and grown over. The mudslide was a steep green meadow. Extraordinary that all the action of seal

159

habitation should leave no trace, no corpse, not a single bone. Now it was the seabirds' season with all the outcry of gulls and the litter of gull-eaten corpses and feathers and castings. The rocks and boulders along the shore now belonged to black guillemots; charming birds, so neat in black and white, crimson of foot and shiny black of bill. I counted thirty-one in a few minutes, ashore and offshore. From each beak swung one of those particular long, red, flattened fishes which a black guillemot seems never to be without. They kept fluttering in from the sea, waddled on the boulders, and whined, and swung their fishes. Their nesting crevices were given away by plentiful whitewash. I hauled out one or two of the fat grey-speckled fledglings for inspection.

We wandered along past Shinglebank and Book Rocks to the straggling wire and posts of the sheep fank. Gullyguard, the area of loose dry boulders at the head of the rocks beyond Fank Gully and on to Island Gully, seemed the likeliest place for petrels, indeed the only place that I could think of apart from possible crevices in the cliffs. So it turned out. The heaps of yellow lichened boulders and stones looked lifeless enough but as soon as we started crawling among them and sniffing we caught the unmistakable whiff of petrel. As soon as we started shifting stones the bird below started that engaging croaking only to be heard from underground. It scuffled out into my hand and sicked-up oil; the pale egg was just within sight. It was as pleasing as ever to have a storm petrel in hand again, to admire those miniature black webbed feet, the bright black eye and queer tubed bill. It wouldn't return to its hole, and flew away zig-zagging over the rocks and out to sea. Brian uncovered, and covered up again, four eggs within a square yard, and flew off two more birds. Each egg was laid on the dark gritty earth, either on a pad of stone chips or on bare soil. When it comes to stones the requirements of stormies are exacting: the stones and boulders must be heaped sufficiently deep, they must be big enough to leave adequate passages in between, and the ground below must be well drained. The stones of Gullyguard were made to measure.

The remembered driftwood lay undisturbed on the beach. My useful table, cut from the huge baulk, had weathered white and clean. New grass and even a few flowering orchids were pushing up among the stones and duckboards of the tent floor, but all the drainage ditches remained scoured and bare. A fine clump of thistles had sprouted from the spoil heap beside the earth house. It only wanted finishing! Looking at the great stone blocks I had a sudden vision of myself in gale and rain, straining at them with driftwood levers. A pair of gloves lay loose on the floor, two shrivelled hands.

The tide had come to high water and any shelter was gone. The boat was rolling and pitching all ways, lifting her forefoot at one end and showing her cutaway at the other, tugging the rope cable to near horizontal. We nearly swamped the dinghy getting off, and then had some critical moments with a stumbling engine as we just crabbed clear of the lee shore.

Next time was a month earlier in the season and as different as could be. Brian and I had spent two days at the Shiant Isles in a heatwave. The Minch was glassy. We must get out on the west side, let's go to St Kilda. The sun went down in Novemberish crimson, the haze darkened and thickened as we came through the Sound, the moon turned from yellow to fire-lit copper, and its glittering track turned with it. We anchored at Shillay at midnight, riding the long low swell, and after a restless night were heading out westwards by eight o'clock next morning.

Coming back four days later in poor visibility we got too far to the north before sighting recognizable shore marks and so came down to a novel view of Shillay. She – and surely so well-loved an island should be she – showed first the blunt overhung nose of the northern cliff and then the great fault that splits the island in two looked as if a pair of enormous whales had collided head on, and stuck, and turned to stone, leaving a black rift between their heads. We passed close down the west side cliffs that had so impressed Professor Heddle: gigantic petrified sandwiches, mountains of fossilized pink fish paste, piles of charred and mouldering books. We rounded rough-looking Little Shillay and came into evening peace and quiet. The bay of Shillay was positively lulling

161

after the worries and anchor watches of Village Bay, St Kilda. We didn't bother when the ebb tide swung the boat's stern into weed and she floated in less than an oar's length of water. The last of the breeze fell away.

We went ashore after midnight to call on the storm petrels. The thrift was fresh in flower, colourless in the dusk, bright pink by torchlight. Gullyguard was alive. It's an unfailing delight to sit amongst small dashing petrels, stormies or fork-tails, in a summer night. And what a night it was! The outcry of gulls and oyster catchers had subsided after our intrusion, the sea was silent, the anxieties of seafaring behind us. All the noise came from underground, the churring and exclamatory croaks, like a pondful of frogs. The birds flew thick and fast, bat-like and in silence. There was enough light left in the thick dusk to see their white rumps, to see their near collisions, to follow their narrowing circles until they finally flopped down and scuttled under the stones. When a bird brushed close past one's face one could even smell it. We sat with them for an hour or more and then went back and moved the boat out into deeper water and slept with no thought for an anchor watch.

The calm held. Next morning's mist cut off the hill of Shillay and touched the crown of Little Shillay; a gentle lap along the boat's side, fussy little waves falling over on the sand. A dozen black guillemots floated sociably round the boat, doing nothing. Now was a first chance for landing on Little Shillay. We rowed along, fishing on the way. We were having a short-lived craze for trailing a rubber eel behind the dinghy and catching whopping great lythe. They cooked to cotton wool laced with needles but the livers were good, until we noticed that they were all infested with parasitic worms.

We found a handy creek in the sheltered corner and left the dinghy afloat among boulders with seaweed for fenders. Really, Little Shillay was one of the nicest little islands I'd ever been on! It was craggy but with soil enough for meadows of grass and banks of flowers. Gasker to the north was low and grazed, Haskeir the other way was a sea rock with human history, but Little Shillay was one of those rare scraps of land literally in a state of nature, forever untouched by human hand or human agency. The only grazing was by the barnacle geese whose last winter's droppings now lay dried and bleached on short grass.

Little Shillay is ninety feet high and about three hundred yards long, north to south. Cliffs face the Atlantic on the west side but the fall of land towards Shillay is gentler, and was full of summer flowers. The foot of the cliffs was a-boil with breaking swell but round the corner was lovely and quiet. The island was busy with birds, gulls and shags, rock pigeons in a cave, eider ducks, black guillemots, rock pipits, oyster catchers. Fulmars sat on their eggs embowered with thrift and mayweed and sweet smelling white campion. Higher up and brighter than the flowers puffins stood in front of their burrows. All alive-oh and not a trace of humanity!

Shillay herself was full of flowers in summertime. The last primroses flowered in the dunes, the last yellow flags on the mudslide. The sward behind the dunes was now a little patch of genuine machair, a sweet smelling carpet of yellow and white, of buttercups and daisies, clover and bedstraw, horseshoe vetch and pink-flowered centaury. The turf was threaded with the stems and silvery leaves of creeping willow; beds of silverweed bordered the dry ponds beyond. The close sea plantain sward of the Lowlands was dotted overall with ragged robin and patches of thrift. Fresh goose droppings showed that summer greylags took over from the barnacle geese of winter. Scabious and orchids flowered up the hill, thyme found its place at each rock edge. The sun had been glaring at the mist and now it broke through hot and strong; the mist vanished into thin air and larks rose into pale blue sky. I sat on the table on the tent floor while the sun warmed my bare back. All that other season of frustration and failure seemed like a separate existence; all I could feel was that I was glad to have seen it through – here.

My drainage works had transformed a little patch of hillside. Peaty sedge had magically changed to a close grazed sward of white clover. The sweetening of shell sand blown up from the beach was there and waiting, all that was wanting was a little elementary drainage. Why didn't the Mackenzies bring out a party of men and put in a day's work with spades? My massive tent pegs were rubbing posts, worn smooth and greasy by sheep.

We dashed from the beach and plunged into green translucent water, but Hebridean bathing was as instant as ever. I went digging at the edge of the dunes, at the old bothy or whatever it was, where two artifact lines of stones showed through the sand. More practical digging had kept me busy before. I got down to a paved floor and found fragments of wood and charcoal, a bit of china and lumps of rust that had once been iron.

We sailed back to Leverburgh in warm evening sunshine and returned next day fuelled and provisioned. Brief summer was ending: sea fog began to drift, the sun lost heart and was soon obscured in doubt and then in certainty. A cold northerly wind sprang up and summer took no time at all to turn to winter. By time we anchored at Shillay visibility was down to a hundred yards and the rigging was dripping with condensed fog. When we went dinghy fishing at midnight storm petrels were fluttering round as if lost. Next morning we did some more stone sniffing: any loose stone anywhere in the island was occupied. Fog swirled round the cliffs, fulmars were riding the currents that also carried up the smell of their colonies below. All that was left for Shillay weather was to see the island in a blizzard of snow.

I continued my digging in the dunes but gave up as soon as I found a teaspoon. It was only an old sheep fank after all (but it might have been something else before that).

Cold wet blowing fog lasted for a night and a day and another night; we left as soon as we could see the way.

Once again the black guillemots were perched along the shoreside rocks and swinging their red fishes. But this time — fresh otter tracks on the sand, a new colony of terns established along the head of the beach. After four more years the rafters of Dune House had fallen in and the pit had drifted full of sand. The earth house had been built up into a cairn and whitewashed for a seamark by the surveyors of HMS *Cook*.

The west end of Island Gully, the cleft that cuts off Angelica Isle from the Lowlands, had always been a cauldron in autumn. Now it was a deep, green pool between rock walls, only connected to the sea by an underwater passage. Two seals, a cow and a scarred old bull, were passing their time there, seeming to enjoy themselves doing nothing noisily, puffing and blowing and bubbling, and staring back at me as if sightlessly. When I stood up and broke the skyline they dived explosively in a desperate twist and splash. I could see them looking up at me from under water. As soon as I lay down they surfaced and went on contentedly puffing and blowing; their hind flippers swayed gently to and fro like seaweed in the tide.

Animals like these, and the usual dozen or so to be seen round the island in summertime, would presumably be first ashore in the autumn. A few more were scattered through the Sound. But where were all the rest? Going about the islands in the *Heather* we would come across odd groups here and there, mostly smallish animals lying out on rocks and skerries. An islet in Loch Claidh and another at the head of Loch Brollum in the east side of Lewis were favourite places for half a dozen, so was the skerry close off Eilean Mhuire of the Shiant Isles. One couldn't but see their love of hauling out to bask and get dry, to scratch and sleep, but there are nowhere near enough rocks to go round, sheltered and free from interference. So where were they all?

The bulk of the population is supposed to go to sea and live a pelagic life during the summer months, whether they like it or not. But who sees seals' heads bobbing or bottling on the surface? (Bottling is hanging vertically in the water, nose pointing to the sky, asleep or half-asleep.) After all a seal has to breathe and must spend most of its time in contact with air. MacBrayne's steamers plough the Minch yet how often does anyone on board spot a seal's head? Four separate times the *Heather* went out to St Kilda and back. We might spot one seal on the way, or none; sighting a whale was more likely.

165

From the Minch to Rockall, sea and ocean are dotted with fishing boats. But fishermen are busy fishing, or navigating or asleep, goes the argument, they don't notice seals. This is simply not true. Fishermen have nothing else to look at but the sea and look at it they do, and see what they see, and it's not often seals.

Why then are seals seldom seen in the open sea? Because the sea is large and seals' heads are small. 'If the seals are not in inshore waters or on the haul-outs, they *must* be farther out at sea,' wrote Professor Hewer, with something like despair between his lines. But even allowing that mortality is heaviest in the seals' first year and can amount to a fearsome 60% (so it is estimated), there is still an annual total of some 30,000 seals of all ages to account for from the breeding stations of Scotland alone . . .

The *Heather*'s last cruise of all also saw her, and my and Brian's last visit to Shillay. Having come back from the mainland and Skye to a last anchorage in the Basin we came along the length of the new channel on as drab and drizzly a day as could be. Every hill was cut off short, the land was as grey as the sea. On such a day peat and stone merely aid and abet the overhead gloom, only shell sand and machair alleviate. Shillay's little seaside garden of sand and flowers made as brave an oasis as ever.

As usual the stock of sheep had been taken off earlier in the summer and the island was being rested until the autumn, except that the Mackenzies had landed a few steers for a trial. The noisy tern colony continued along the beach head but nosy hard-breathing steers treading among the eggs had brought a new hazard. The usual few big seals interested themselves in our visit, the storm petrels' stones smelt as they should, the black guillemots were all on station. The whitewash had already weathered from the stones of the earth house; the tent peg posts were as solid as ever; my tiny bright green patch of Improved Grazing remained a living mark. We set off on the last lap back to Stornoway.

The Sound of Harris remains a safe place to go back to.

Nothing much has changed or is likely to change. Red Rock and Sgeir Innes, Girls Rock and The Irishman still lead to Shillay.